From Home-Based to **POWERHOUSE**

Strategies to Take Your Travel Passion to Profit

By Anita Pagliasso

From Home-Based to POWERHOUSE

5453 Silver Vista Way, San Jose, CA 95318
408.531.9228

Editing by Salle Hayden www.upstartservices.com

Cover design, layout and production by Ken Flores
Ken Flores Graphic Design and Art Design
408.386.9844 kflores1@mac.com

ISBN-10 0615468349
ISBN-13 9780615468341

ACCOLAIDES

Anita Pagliasso is an innovative, creative and crackerjack travel marketer who practices what she preaches in her own travel agency. As a columnist for Agent @ Home magazine for the past five years, she's been providing great advice to agents working from home. Now she outdoes herself in her new book, which is an essential read for home-based travel agents seeking to grow their business and anyone who wants to effectively market and sell travel

James Shillinglaw, Editor in Chief, Agent @ Home Magazine

Anita Pagliasso is mentor for many travel agents. Her expertise in operating and promoting a successful travel business has been admired and respected by many travel educators. Her ability to provide agents with the knowledge and tools to become a successful home based agent is priceless. OSSN recommends her books and training materials to new and veteran agents.

Gary Fee, President, OSSN www.ossn.com

Success guru Tony Robbins says that if you want to be successful, model yourself on someone who has already achieved the success you seek. When it comes to succeeding as a home-based travel agent, I can think of no better role model than Anita Pagliasso. She's a rock star and a total inspiration. I recommend her books to all my students.

Kelly Monaghan, CTC, **HomeTravelAgency.com**

Anita Pagliasso has the magic marketing formula which has propelled her to unparalleled levels of success as a home-based agency and Celebrity Cruises. Anita's vision, creativity, practical marketing tactics, and proven experience as a powerful and successful retailer and marketer make Anita Pagliasso a true winner and one of a kind in the home-based agency community. Anita's workshops, books, and articles have helped thousands of home-based agents build their business and increase their client base with new opportunities and leads. Celebrity Cruises is lucky to have Anita and Ticket to Travel on our winning team. Agents everywhere can benefit from Anita's winning formula of success.

Cris De Souza, Channel Strategy Executive, Celebrity Cruises/Azamara Cruises Sales Department – www.celebrity.com– www.azamara.com

"I have had the pleasure of knowing and working with Anita for over 15 years. Her book, " How I Made a Small Fortune as a Home Based Agent" and CD, "Tool Box for Home Based Agents" have been part of Career Quest's training programs for new travel agents. Anita has conducted marketing seminars for Career Quest over the years and is a frequent speaker on our monthly chat rooms. Many of our graduates have chosen "A Ticket2Travel" as their host agency and all we ever hear are raves about the support Anita provides her agents. On behalf of Career Quest, I wish Anita the best of luck with her new book."

Nancy Kist, CTC President of Career Quest Training Center

I have been an avid traveler for as far back as I can remember. So I thought it was a natural transition when I was invited to work in a travel agency. The next step would be to open my own agency! Very soon I realized that a traveler and a successful travel agent are two very different animals. How I would have loved to get my hands on Anita Pagliasso's books back then!

In both my work as a travel agent and working with people with disabilities over the last twenty four years, I have met few people as dedicated and caring as the author of this book. She has helped many navigate the complex field of selling travel successfully and fulfilling their dreams of a profitable business. She has a large fan following who are convinced of her competence as well as her ability to motivate and educate.

Unlike her previous books, this new book "From Home-Based to POWERHOUSE! Marketing strategies to take your passion to profit" is a big step of accomplishment by a home-based agent. She shares her coming of age in the industry with insightful, innovative, and creative marketing ideas. It is a must read book for anyone who wants to have fun selling travel and keep the cash registers running too. We, at SATH (Society for Accessible Travel & Hospitality), strongly recommend anyone planning an entry into the travel business, or who has been in it for a long time, to read this book and get their businesses to flourish. This beautifully written book will not only guide you through the intricate web of creative and successful marketing, but also will instill more passion into your selling.

Jani Nayar, Executive Coordinator, SATH
(Society for Accessible Travel & Hospitality) www.sath.org/

When Anita became part of the travel scene in 1992, home-based travel agents were a new phenomenon. Many independent agents were struggling for the same respect and acceptance that their colleagues who worked in brick and mortar agencies enjoyed. Anita played a major part in showing the world what home-based agents could do. She successfully started her own travel business and she led the growth of the San Jose/Bay Area Chapter of the Outside Sales Support Network through its early years. She continues to direct this chapter and is currently the Western Regional Manager as well. Through her hands-on textbooks, her seminars at industry events, and her leadership and marketing skills Anita has opened many doors for new agents and given stature to the home-based concept throughout the USA. Loving the travel industry and wanting to share her insights and expertise with others is a high priority with Anita. She is an enthusiastic sponsor of the Foothill College Travel

Careers Program, serving on our Advisory board and giving seminars and workshops. Foothill deeply appreciates the energy and enthusiasm that Anita exudes in everything she does.

Sharon Hack, CTC DS, Director, Foothill College Travel Careers

Anita is a successful POWERHOUSE who has taken her passion and turned it into huge profits. Take advantage of this opportunity to learn the secrets to how you too can be successful in your own travel business. This book is your map to making a profit as a home-based travel agent.

As in travel, without a map, you are destined to get lost and lose time and money. We highly recommend this book to keep you on course and get you to your destination … a profitable travel business. Anita has always stood out from the crowded travel business marketplace. She is professional, dynamic and extraordinarily creative. Jump on this opportunity to learn how to harness some of her experience to become a more profitable home-based business.

Keith and Martha Powell – Business Revivalist – Powell Speaks

I wanted to touch base to let you know that your continual attitude of going after the business is appreciated! I've used your articles as lessons for our Sales Team.

In this economy, agents who "get it" and realize that they are truly salespeople will be the ones who reap the rewards. You've written great things and from one sales professional to another – keep up the "sales attitude" – we make the World go around!

Mark Junette, VP of Sales, Contiki, www.contiki.com

Anita inspires me to be creative and unique. The day I got her first book I fixed a cup of coffee and read it cover to cover that night. It's the best purchase I ever made for marketing purposes. She tells you how to stand out from the crowd, how to create travel guides for her clients, and how to market in the most innovative ways. I can't thank her enough for all of her fantastic, creative ideas. And her new book is not only more of the same, but lots of new ideas, too. She's the best!

Tish Black-Hughes, Anytime Travel, anytimetravel@insightbb.com

The Author | ANITA PAGLIASSO

Anita Pagliasso started her career in travel in 1992 after switching gears from selling electronic components in the heart of Silicon Valley, California. Because of her own love of travel her home eventually became a travel library filled with file cabinets full of travel information. Soon friends and family began calling on her for her expertise and she became a home-based travel consultant. Since then she has built a flourishing, successful business by standing out from the crowd and getting noticed.

In 1993 Anita was appointed as the San Jose Chapter Director for OSSN (Outside Sales Support Network). OSSN is a networking organization that was formed in 1990 to provide support, education and further the professionalism of the home-based travel agent. Under Anita's helm the San Jose/Bay Area OSSN Chapter went on to become the largest in the organization and still remains the flagship chapter. Additionally, in 1995 Anita was named OSSN's Western Regional Manager and in 2009 their National Conference Director. She has received numerous awards from OSSN for her efforts.

Anita has produced numerous seminars based on the content of her publications and also makes regular presentations to various colleges and travel education forums as well as at most major travel industry conferences. She also produced the "30 Second Marketing Course" for Princess Cruise Line's One Source Academy.

Anita is a monthly columnist for Agent@Home Magazine. She has also had numerous articles written about her success in publications such as; Income Opportunities Magazine, Travel Weekly, Travel Agent, Travel Age West, San Jose Mercury News, Saturday Evening Post and the New York Times.

She is the author of the popular book **How I Made a Small Fortune as a Home-Based Travel Agent** where the author/speaker shares her knowledge, expertise and proven techniques with readers. The book is filled with fun and innovative marketing ideas as well as sample letters and forms she has developed over the years. Also included are tips on how to overcome the diversions, distractions and objections of working from home. All the pros and cons of running a home-based business are covered in this comprehensive and insightful book. Anita has also produced a CD, **"Anita's Tool Box for Home-Based Travel Agents,"** which includes dozens of the forms, documents and sample letters that you will need to run a successful home-based travel business. (www.redticketproductions.com)

Table of Contents

Introduction | Home-Based to POWERHOUSE

From Home-Based to POWERHOUSE is a blend of frankness, facts, honesty all combined with a bit of humor. You will learn the "how to" along with real stories about how I took my own travel business from a passion for travel to a successful and profitable business.

Some home-based agents may wonder what their future holds as the media continually casts doom and gloom on the travel industry. Judging by the number of new inquiries I receive from those who are passionate about the prospect of getting into the business of selling travel, I can honestly say that I think that our future is bright.

Over 30 million Americans currently operate some type of business from their homes. This growth and acceptance has spilled over into the travel industry over the last decade. Even traditional Brick-and-Mortar agencies have found that they can take their business home and eliminate the unnecessary financial burden of the overhead involved with operating out of a storefront.

Throughout the book you will discover the benefits of running a successful, and yes – profitable, home-based business. My wish is that you will find this book easy to follow and that it will include plenty of practicable and attainable advice to set you on your own road to success.

Please read on to learn how to run a real business, making real money, with the respect of a CEO all from your passion of travel.

Much success to you!

Part I

BUILDING A POWERHOUSE

Chapter 1 | WHY IT PAYS TO WORK FROM HOME

NO PLACE LIKE HOME - *NO TIME LIKE NOW*

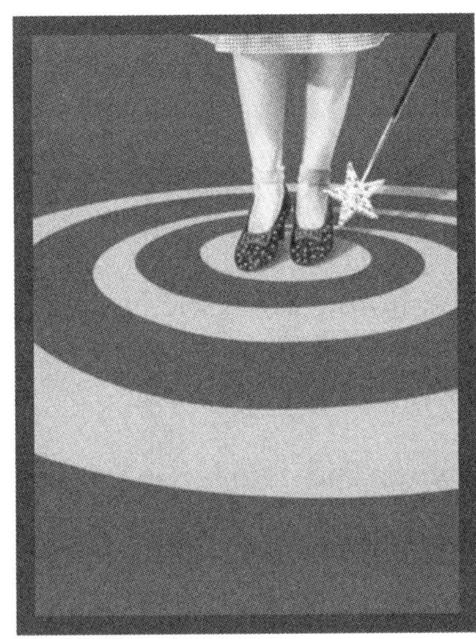

If you are looking to get out of the rat race, spend more time with family and friends, and live a more balanced life, a home-based travel business may be the right decision for you.

I will cover some of these rewards and risks in further detail throughout the book but here are some reasons why it pays to work from home:

Personal freedom – If you're used to spending hours in traffic to and from work every day, some of the most exciting advantages of starting a home-based business are your new-found freedom and retrieval of lost time. According to the U.S. Federal Highway Administration, the average American spends 348 hours each year commuting. With a home-based business, suddenly you have those extra hours to regain control of your personal life. Plus, there are no bosses, no dress code, no set work schedule, and no office politics. All you will need is personal drive, discipline, marketing, and time-management skills.

You get to keep the money you make – Really, it's a simple principle! Your earnings potential is directly proportional to your performance, so there is no waiting for a raise or a promotion. The harder you work, the more you will produce. You'll also save money in areas such as gas and food. Preparing lunch at home is more cost efficient and also offers a nice break in your workday.

Increased opportunity – With so many corporations and industries in a slump, starting your own home-based travel agency means you can create your own income producing opportunities. Good job prospects can be scarce in some industries, and promotional opportunities in major companies are also shrinking. With many now opting to take early retirement packages, becoming an agent is an excellent chance to take your passion for travel and turn it into a second career.

Less risk – Running a travel business from home takes much less start up cash than starting a store-front business- or even a franchise location. Since there is no inventory or products to purchase, and the business is located where you reside. There aren't the additional monthly expenses of rent, leases, or utilities.

More time for friends and family – This is especially important for parents of school age children. You can see the kids off to school, and on most days, be home when they return. Also, if someone is sick, it's easier to leave your desk rather than in the corporate office.

Less stress – It's a little less stressful to juggle the demands of work and family when you know that you can stay home to care for a sick child. Generally you can also make appointments according to your set schedule. Also, it's best to try to schedule multiple appointments on the same day to coincide with other events on your calendar. Example: If your weekly networking meeting is on Tuesday, set as many other appointments as possible for that same day, even if it's a trip to the dry cleaners.

Opportunities for professional growth – Being your own boss gives you the chance to wear lots of hats: sales director, marketing professional, strategist, business development manager, and more. This gives insight and familiarity with all the aspects of running a business.

Increased productivity – Now that you no longer have to budget time and energy for commuting or attending a succession of useless meetings, you should have a lot more time and energy to make your business a success.

A creative outlet – Launching your home-based agency can be an opportunity for you to give birth to your passion and create money-generating opportunities by using your creativity for trying new ideas, taking risks, and running the business exactly how you want.

No inventory – With selling travel, unlike Mary Kay Cosmetics or other home-based business models, there is no need to purchase or maintain inventory. Brochures and documents are provided by the suppliers. This means you don't need to worry about anything but making the sale.

Work from Home – You don't need the overhead of a corporate office for this type of business. You can run it right out of your home. Long gone is the perception that home-based travel agents were thought to be somehow less professional than their storefront counterparts. Today, suppliers actively seek out home-based travel agents and are considered to be the most sought after segment of the travel industry.

Flexible Hours – You can work the hours you choose. If you have a full-time job, you can work your business in the evenings and on weekends. If you're a stay-at-home mom, you can run it when the kids are at school. And if your child gets sick, you can take a day off.

Tax advantages – There are a number of tax advantages to having your home and office under one roof. Check with your tax advisor to see if they recommend deducting a part of your home's operating and depreciation expenses as business expenses. This can be a percentage of your mortgage, property taxes, insurance, utilities, and/or the expenses of household maintenance.

Personal Growth and Development – The nature of the type of selling you will be doing in this business puts you in contact with many and varied individuals. Over time, your sales and developmental skills will become ever more finely honed. You will develop a great deal of personal satisfaction from helping your travel clients.

9 to 5'ers Traffic Jam
STOP

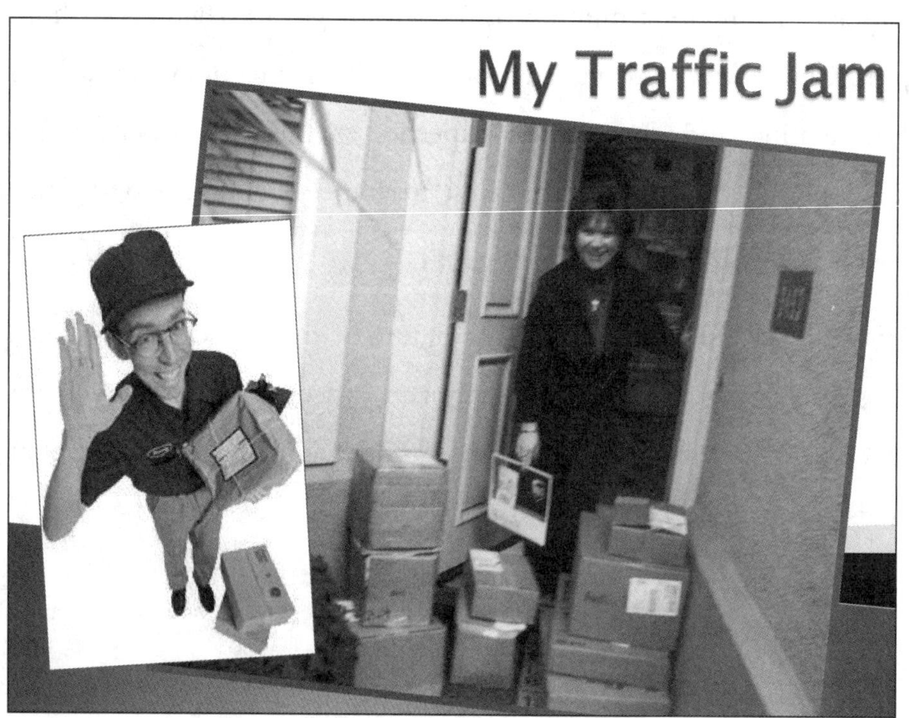
My Traffic Jam

Chapter 2 | PREPARING FOR BUSINESS

Are you looking for new business? Think of your search for new clients for your business as a job or project, just like you would if you were unemployed and starting out to look for work. Begin by getting yourself organized and make a list of potential employers or "clients" who you think you would like to work for.

WRITE A RESUME

Whether or not you give this to a client, it's an excellent exercise in learning about yourself and your own qualifications as a travel consultant. If you haven't done a resume for quite a while, you can find lots of sample forms on Google. Chances are that during this process you will clarify your qualifications as a travel consultant. What an employer (your potential clients) really wants to know is how you excelled at past jobs. They want to know about your achievements.

How would you answer the following on your resume?

- How do you stand out among others who have held the same job?
- Did you make or save the employer (your clients) money?
- Did you initiate any new procedures that improved service?

Getting new business can be just like going through a job search process

GET TO KNOW THE COMPETITION

Make a list of 10 things that really make you stand out from your competition? Do you deliver documents to their home or office? Are you available evenings and weekends for consultations? Maybe you are an Africa Wildlife Specialist or Incentive Travel Consultant. One of my agents does fund-raising cruises for organizations, and another specializes in cruises for caregivers. Whatever it is that sets you apart should be on your list.

CREATE A PORTFOLIO

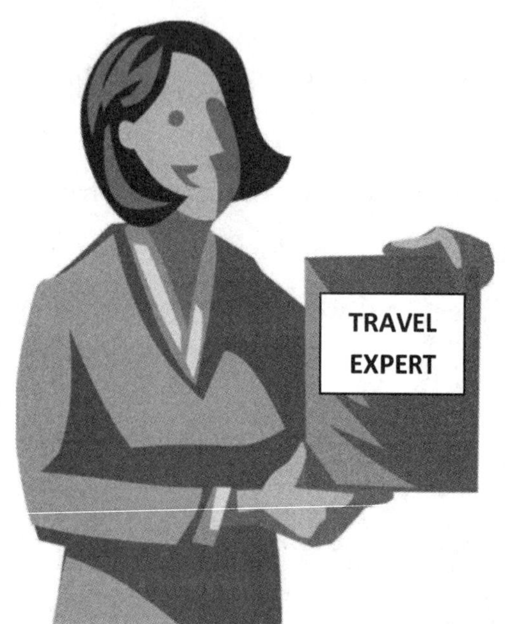

Are your walls in your office covered with certificates of achievement? Perhaps you have completed your Certified Travel Counselor (CTC) accreditation, or you have become a Princess Commodore, a Sandals Specialist, or possibly a CLIA Accredited Cruise Counselor (ACC). If they are not on your walls, they may be tucked away in a drawer or file somewhere. Why not display these achievements in a way that will help you get the job? I took all of my certificates and put them in a very nice album that I always take with me when I meet with potential new clients. I have also included articles that I have written on various destinations that I've visited. I review the contents on a regular basis to remove outdated articles or update certificates. This has worked tremendously well because it gives the clients a visual and professional image of me and my qualifications.

PREPARE FOR THE INTERVIEW

Just as in any job interview, you wouldn't talk about salary before the end of interview process. Discuss your qualifications first and why you think you are best suited for the job. Then, find out exactly what are the expectations of your potential employer (your client). The very last step would be quoting prices.

DETAIL YOUR QUALIFICATIONS

Learn how to give rapid-fire answers to why a client should give you the job. List all of the common questions that may be asked of you, such as, "Why should I book with you rather than over the internet?" One of my answers would be this: "I will work with you on a personal one-on-one basis throughout the planning process and through your welcome home to make sure you get exactly what you want. If you use an Internet source, you will most likely never talk to the same agent twice.

> *"If you want to be taken seriously as a business, you have to look, act and dress professionally."*

Another question might be, "Aren't you more expensive?" My answer: "Actually, in many cases I offer prices that are lower than the Internet because I have access to many sources and have established preferred supplier relations to make sure you are getting the best price." I also mention specific times when I have saved a client's vacation because I was available to intervene on their behalf when a problem occurred during a trip. Don't be afraid to mention the various horror stories that you have heard about Internet bookings that have gone horribly wrong. Remember, this interview period may be your only chance. Make sure you come across confident, experienced and eager to get the job!

PORTRAY A PROFESSIONAL IMAGE

If you want to be taken seriously as a business, you have to look, act and dress professionally. I know that we are in the business of selling fun, but it is still a business…and it's *your* business. When I go to conferences on selling luxury travel, I am always amazed to see travel agents show up in shorts and flip flops. Invest in one nice suit or, at the minimum, get some quality casual business wear with YOUR brand or logo on it.

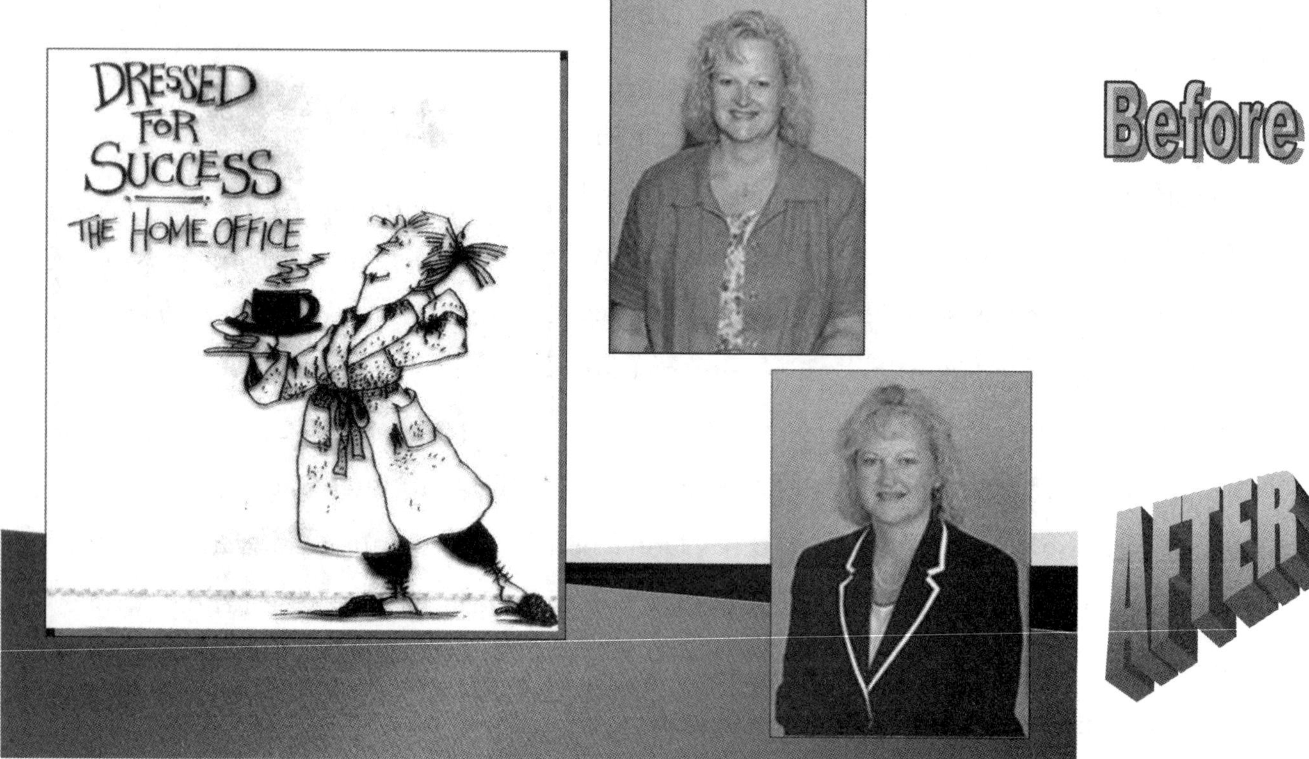
DRESSED
FOR
SUCCESS
THE HOME OFFICE
Before
AFTER

Chapter 3 | MANAGING HOME & BUSINESS

JUGGLING ACT

Working from home is a balancing act. Picture yourself on a unicycle in the middle of a circus ring, holding a stack of plates in your arms. Then, imagine throwing those plates high above your head. Some of them are the roles you play as a businessperson; others are various clients that can be requiring your attention all at the same time. And, finally, there are all of the little plates that represent the different aspects of your everyday personal life. If you're new to the art of juggling, you will probably drop a few – or even taking a tumble...

To say that running a home-based travel business is a juggling act is an understatement. First, there are all the roles you play in your business, from president to janitor. Second, there is the possibility of having multiple travel bookings from several clients. While that all sounds wonderful, it requires a host of skills to keep them separate and on schedule, while trying to give each your full attention to detail, while simultaneously needing to work on something else. Finally, there are all the parts that ongoing marketing requires, such as networking meetings, interviews with new clients, researching trips, and updates for websites and social networking, to mention a few. You need two principal skills keep all those plates in the air: intense concentration and the ability to switch gears on a dime.

Continue to fill the pipeline – Each aspect of work presents its own challenges but none so much as having enough work to keep one financially afloat. It can be a real struggle to land enough good clients to sustain you. Then, when you have the client, it can take up a lot of your time and energy, to the detriment of finding more work once their travel booking is complete. The "secret" of always having work is to be always looking for it – in other words, engaging in an ongoing marketing effort. The key words here are organized and ongoing. No matter how much you have to do, keeping that pipeline filled should be your top priority.

Respect deadlines – For our business, it's critical to meet deadlines. If a client's payment needs to be made we can't fall back on excuses. But what happens when you are working with multiple clients or groups at the same time? This is when organization, check lists and reminders are crucial. There have been times when I feel that I'm in a whirlwind and fret that I may miss a deadline. I started treating my calendar and reminders like I treat my alarm clock. I know that if it's urgent not to miss an important appointment, I set the alarm early and then a second alarm as a backup. Whenever possible, I always give my client's a deposit or final payment date that's a week or so earlier that what is actually needed by the supplier. Create your own reliable back up plan.

Every plate is important – People remember the smallest details: you didn't return a call; you made a promise you didn't keep; your voice mail was full, and they couldn't leave a message; you sounded less than warm when you answered your phone; your handshake was limp. You are always "on," even when you may not realize it. Your voice reveals your state of mind; your clothes position you; your grooming speaks to your attention to detail. Get the idea? Everything counts!

Who moved your priorities? – There are times when no matter how organized or single focused you attempt to be, your proprieties will get shifted. You know the scenario… your workday is running fairly smoothly and manageable. You feel like you are getting a handle on things. You're answering emails, checking off your to-do list, calling in client payments when suddenly you get a call that requires you to handle a client's travel emergency, oftentimes taking hours of your day to resolve. It's unrealistic to expect that there won't be obstacles that come in that will prevent you from keeping schedules. What sometimes feels like a circus within the realm of running a business, we catch the flaming batons, put out the fires, and then jump back on the unicycle and start juggling again.

Balancing and juggling your life as a work-at-home agent is not easy. But you don't have to manage your business in such a circus-like manner. It takes work and tenacity in your commitment. It involves strategizing and the willingness to be flexible. In fact, flexibility is a must. But after a while, you will develop the skills to best keep all of your plates in the air.

TIME MANAGEMENT

One of the most challenging aspects of running a home-based business is the matter of managing time effectively. Many of us feel there are just not enough hours in the day. Don't beat yourself up.

Think about all of the hats that you wear on a daily basis.

- Marketing manager
- Sales manager
- Customer and supplier relationships
- Accounts payable
- Accounts receivable
- Advertising and promotions
- Data entry and maintenance
- Correspondence / office administrator
- Janitor

If this hasn't made you reach for your bottle of Excedrin, also take into consideration the fact that you still need to make time for family obligations and other social activities.

CLUTTER CONTROL

Often the biggest time waster comes about when the office is unorganized and cluttered. A lot of time can be wasted when looking for a misplaced file or a brochure or how about that important note that you scribbled on the back of a used envelope you pulled out of the waste basket? To help eliminate too much clutter in my home-office, I have put the majority of the file cabinets in the garage. I have narrower storage cabinets with doors on one side of the garage that hold office supplies, brochures, travel guides, books, etc. These types of cabinets are fairly inexpensive and easy to assemble. It's nice to have all the brochures and supplies behind doors. The brochures are then put in labeled magazine holders and arranged by destination.

KEEPING UP WITH THE INDUSTRY

Trade publications are an excellent means of keeping current of what is happening in the ever-changing travel industry. A lot of these magazines are published weekly so it can be difficult to keep up with them and not allow them to pile up. But stopping to read them when the mail arrives takes time away from other important tasks. I now put them straight from the mail into a tote bag that I take with me on flights, to doctor visits and any other appointments where I know I will have a wait time.

PAJAMA PARTY!

When you work at home, it's all about freedom of choice

Are you sitting at work in your PJs today? Did you know that there's actually a "National Wear Your Pajamas to Work Day"? I didn't either until I stumbled upon the official website. It says that originally the "National Wear Your Pajamas to Work Day" was always the day after taxes are due in the United States."

As agents who work from home, we're fortunate to have the luxury of celebrating this awesome day any day of the year that we want! This freedom of choice in wardrobe does not stop at working at home in your pajamas – it extends to every aspect of your business.

I know what it's like to work at home, so pajamas and sweats are kind of a staple of my wardrobe as I begin many of my days. Thinking back to my years of business suits and pumps, it's nice to feel good about the fact that I can wear whatever I want in the comfort of my own home office. I can wake up in the morning, make coffee and, thanks to available technology, sit down in front of a laptop in my own kitchen to start helping clients and making money.

But working in your boxers or nighties doesn't necessarily mean you have to go to your computer straight from bed, complete with disheveled hair and drool running down your cheek. To keep my self-discipline, I go for an early walk, take a shower and try to get to my desk by 7:30 or 8 a.m.

Unless you're Hugh Hefner, "working in your PJs" does not necessarily mean literally wearing pajamas. I'm never exactly dressed to the nines when I'm sitting at my desk, but any sort of comfortable clothing will do, such as a jogging suit or a T-shirt and jeans. At least I try to wear something suitable so that I can answer the door when the postman knocks.

Industry acceptance has opened a whole new lifestyle for countless people who want to run a travel business from home. But working in your PJs doesn't mean you're less productive than a suit-and-tie person. You're being practical, and you're enjoying the flexibility that working at home affords you. So here are some tips to being comfortable and productive:

End the guilty feelings – Working from home means never having to call in sick. You can start later in the day without taking a whole day off because you woke up with a headache. You can have that three-hour lunch with an old friend. No one's watching your clock to make sure you don't take an extra 15 minutes. Spend more time with your children, your husband or partner. Watch your children and grandchildren grow and don't miss their milestone moments. You can do it all, without your boss wondering where your priorities are.

You decide what's important and what's urgent. You run your own schedule and change it at the blink of an eye.

Work at your own pace – If you don't get something done, you don't fret about it. You can always go back to work whenever you have the opportunity to do so. You decide what's important and what's urgent. You run your own schedule and change it at the blink of an eye. You can work at home during the hours that make the most sense for you. Maybe you're not a nine-to-five person. When you work at home you can work six to two, or midnight to five in the morning, if that suits you. When you work at home, you can schedule your days off and vacations on your own schedule. Appointments can be arranged at your most convenient time and place. The only thing that restricts your flexibility is the need to meet your customers' important needs and keep outside commitments.

Decide where to work in your pajamas – Working from home is portable. While most traditional storefront agents work from behind their desks, we can work from the road.

How about working in those pineapple-print pajamas from the balcony of your Hawaiian hotel?

Save the planet – When you work at home, you never have to fight traffic to get to work on time. Your longest commute is from your bedroom to your desk. That means you will save on gas and help the fight against global warming.

If, like me, you're working from home today, be grateful that every day can be a "National Wear Your Pajamas to Work Day." And if you're caught in your PJs at three o'clock in the afternoon, you can simply explain that you're celebrating a holiday! Working at home is not about getting to live your whole life wearing pajamas, it's about freedom of choice, and that is a truly priceless commodity.

FLEXIBILITY AND CONTROL

A benefit of working from the home is that you have the flexibility to set your own hours and the availability to schedule appointments to fit your personal and business needs. What we sometimes forget is that we must discipline ourselves to control and manage our schedules and calendars.

Ways to make your home-based work day more productive, efficient and flexible

Nothing seems to upset my work flow as much as having to leave the office. When I return to the office it always seems difficult to get back into the swing of productivity. What I have learned to do is manage my calendar better and schedule all out of the office appointments so that I can cluster all out-of-the-office appointments. For example, I know that every week I have a Chamber of Commerce meeting on Wednesday at noon, so, whenever possible, I schedule all other out of the office appointments around that event on Wednesday. I also make appointments during non-commute hours to avoid the wasted time in traffic jams.

FREEDOM'S TEMPTATIONS

Working from the privacy of your home gives you the freedom to run the business exactly how you want. You can work the hours you want, schedule your appointments to suit your needs and adjust your hours to fit in personal appointments.

But with freedom also come temptations.

- Get dressed or stay in your sweats or pajamas
- Sleep in late or …stay up late
- Oprah or Dr. Phil
- Snacking and overeating
- Tending to the laundry and other household chores
- Procrastinating
- Naps in the afternoon
- Or…just plain working too much!

Some days I do just fine with this freedom and then there are days that I long for more structure and not so many choices.

You will need to develop reliable self-management and motivational skills that will work best for you and your personality. Personally, procrastination is my biggest challenge. I have had to discipline myself to complete projects and mundane tasks before they become critical or overwhelming.

WHEN "WORK IS HOME" AND "HOME IS WORK"

For home-based agents, "Home **IS** Work" and "Work **IS** Home", meaning "You are always at work." As confusing as this sounds is about how conflicting it sometimes feels. There are times when I wished I could "go home from work" but when you have a home office the work is always there. It is important to set reasonable hours for yourself, know when it is time to quit, shut the doors, put up the "CLOSED" sign and "go home."

ACTIVITY VS ACHIEVEMENT

How many of us finish an exhaustive day, then sit back and wonder what we have really accomplished? To eliminate this feeling, I try to go for an "early" walk each morning before I start work. This keeps me healthy and allows me quiet time to mentally compose a list of what I need to do for the upcoming workday. When I get back to the office I write my list of tasks and goals for the day. There is nothing better to achieve a sense of accomplishment then having a list of items to cross off at the end of the day.

"How many of us finish an exhausting day, then sit back and wonder what we have really accomplished?"

FIGHTING THOSE ISOLATION BLUES

I happen to find planning travel very interesting and simulating. After all, that's what originally drew me into the travel business in the first place. I also love the challenges involved of running a home-based business. One issue that most of home-based agents face at some point, however, is the isolation factor of running a business by yourself.

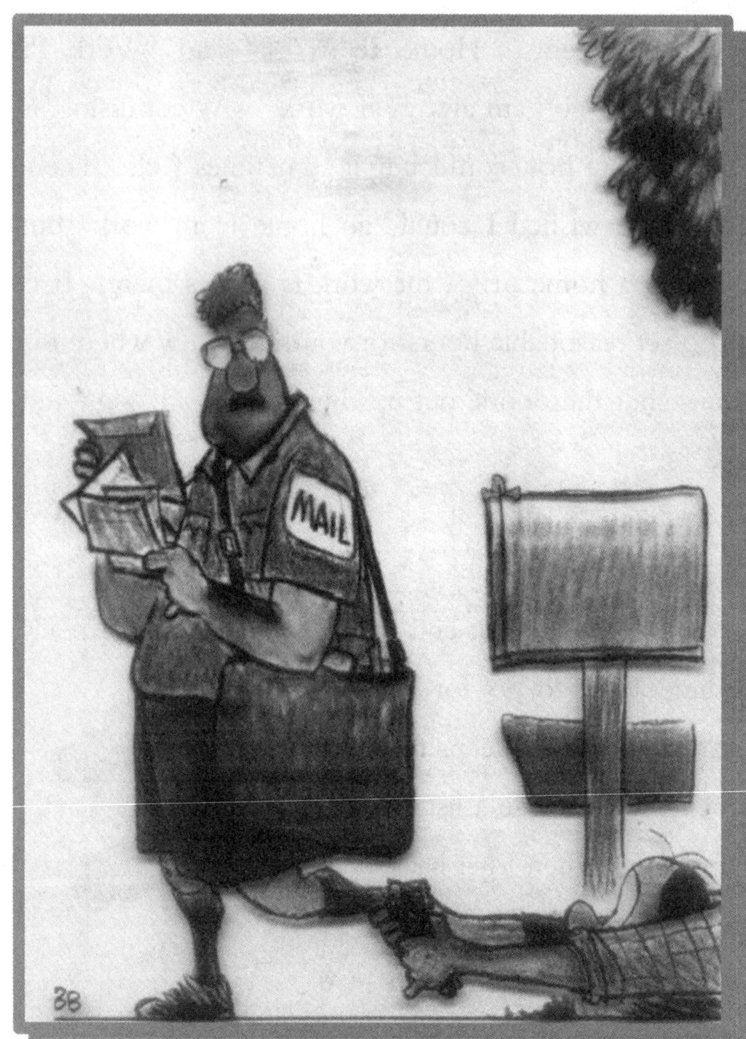

Ways to avoid loneliness and maintain contacts while boosting your home-based business

Running an independent travel business means that most of the time we are living by our client's deadlines. And let's face it, when that client calls and wants that last minute vacation, most of us will work beyond those "normal" business hours to make that sale happen. This often presents challenges when you want to maintain social contacts and still have time to participate in other activities. It is very common to suddenly realize that at the end of the day you are spending the majority of the hours working. While many of us applaud this condition, after all, being busy means business is good, eventually you will realize that there has to be something else in your life before you find yourself inviting the UPS man in for tea and biscuits because you desperately long for a face-to-face conversation with someone.

Some of us love the solitude of being alone all day, while others feel lonely and isolated, and miss the daily social interactions with co-workers. Sometimes you just need a change of scenery, a change of activity, a chance to unhinge from the chair that sometimes feels permanently attached.

ATTEND INDUSTRY EVENTS

To avoid some of the feelings of isolation, I try to regularly attend as many industry and supplier events as time permits. The side benefit to this type of socializing will present opportunities to meet and talk with other home-based agents and to make contacts with various suppliers. Local meetings are a great way to meet the supplier's local Business Development Manager (BDM) or District Sales Manager (DSM).

JOIN PROFESSIONAL ASSOCIATIONS

Professional organizations offer home-based agents some of the best ways to combat isolation, provided there is a local chapter for the group and you attend regular meetings. OSSN is one such association that is geared specifically for home-based agents and has more than 70 of these chapters nationwide. These organizations also can help further your professionalism and education by providing information on current industry issues that affect the home-based travel agent. In addition, such meetings are avenues to network with other local home-based agents to share business ideas and problem-solving solutions.

Associations, such as OSSN offer member-to-member online bulletin boards where home-based agents post questions and receive first-hand knowledge and guidance on almost anything, from where to get good buys on office supplies to destination and supplier recommendations. I have found that even if I don't have any questions I have learned so much just by logging in and reading what other agents are discussing. There are also numerous online chat rooms for agents. Both of these options are great ways to have interactive communication with your peers. I also suggest joining a local Networking group that offers an effective means of linking together with other businesses and through trust and relationship building. These contacts become walking, talking advertisements for you and your business. By doing just this, not only did I meet interesting people, I also increased my business substantially through their referrals.

GET OUT OF THE OFFICE

Most of us who are home-based agents really never stop thinking about business. After all, we never know where our next new client will come from. Since we don't have the luxury of having clients walk through our front door the best way to find them is by getting out among the buyers. Your next biggest client could come from the person on the equipment next to you at the gym, sitting next to you at Starbucks, standing in line at the theatre, working with you at a volunteer event. For this reason I never leave home without a good supply of business cards. Theses outings create a duel benefit…eliminating the feelings of isolation and also exposing yourself to meeting potential new clients. We all need extracurricular activities that not only interest us but also make us more interesting people. The possibility that our outside interests may place us in situations that may present new business opportunities is a huge benefit. So get out of the office when you are feeling lonely or isolated. The fringe benefit is that virtually anyone you meet could be your next new client.

Meet your new associates

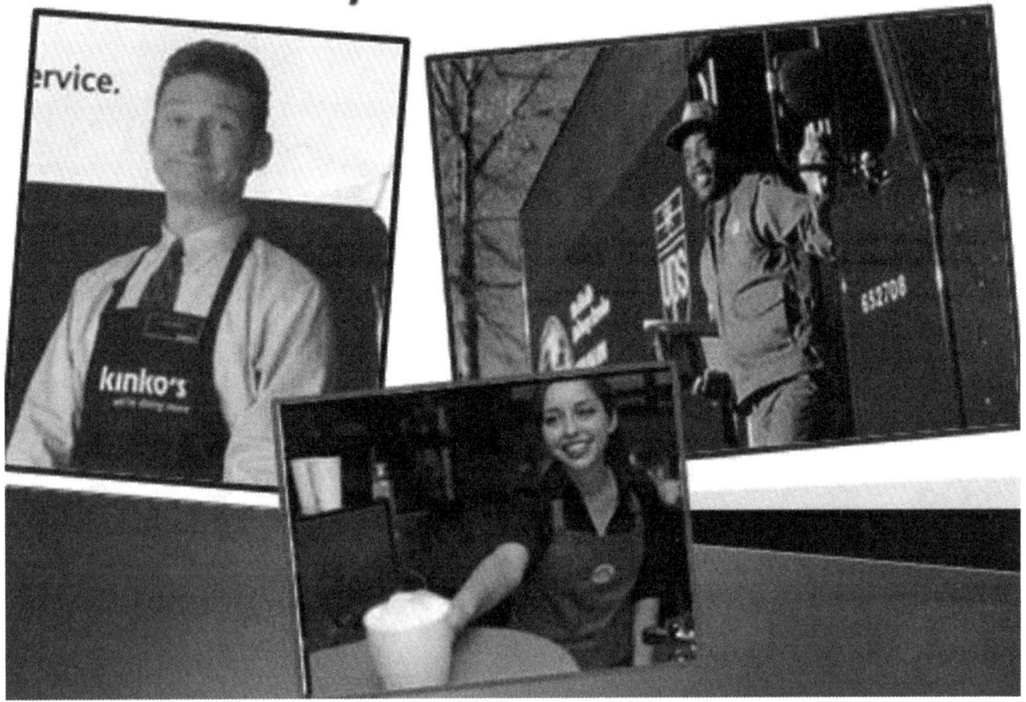

GROWING BEYOND SOLO

One of the reasons I love what I do is that I am constantly challenged to come up with new ideas to grow my business. But along with the success of building a business come added responsibilities and tasks, which at times can be daunting.

Wouldn't it be awesome if we could do only the things that we love to do and have all of the other mundane tasks magically completed, such as entering clients' bookings into a database, balancing the check book and all of your relentless paperwork chores? As your home-based travel business builds, there likely will come a time when you find yourself facing more than you can do on your own. Along with building a successful business comes more work, more responsibility and longer hours. Some days I honestly feel that even if I worked 24 hours a day I would never run out of things to do.

What happens when you grow to that point where you just know that you need help but financially you are not quite ready to take on the expense of hiring someone full time?

Get help! – That help can come in the form of a supportive host agency, an intern from a travel school, a retired person looking for part-time work, a partnership with another agent, a teenage neighbor or even your children or spouse

Family Affair – I know many home-based agents who have turned their business into a family affair. When it's a cooperative effort and everyone pitches in, expenses are cut expenses and everyone shares in the details of running the business.

Among the many agents I've met across the country, I've run into many couples who have formed successful business partnerships around their home-based travel business. Typically one spouse is the "sales and marketing person" and the other is the "organizational" or "detail" person. As in any partnership, to avoid conflict and misunderstandings, responsibilities and objectives should be clearly decided in the beginning.

Junior Achievement – Most of us have children, grandchildren, middle or high-school neighbors who are willing to work for a fairly low price. There are tasks such as stuffing or stamping envelopes, or filing brochures that would be perfectly suited for kids. Heck, just having someone cleaning out and organizing a junk drawer in my office would be a huge favor. *You would be surprised at how many brochures can get filed for the price of a Nintendo game*!

Internships – Go to your local travel school and ask the department head what's required to be accepted into the internship program. Usually these are temporary jobs that require a minimum of 50 hours plus a minimal wage in order to get school credit. You can also contact local career placement and retirement centers. There are many retirees looking for a second career for which this might be an excellent opportunity.

Bookkeeping and Database Entry Services – You may want to consider paying for an outside support service before the demands become overwhelming. Decide how much you want them to handle. A bookkeeping service, for example, can maintain tasks from accounts receivable and payable, put together financial statements to take care of bank reconciliation. Finding help with database entry will depend on how often you provide updates, what program you use, etc. This service is especially helpful after you have collected data from exhibiting at a major bridal fair or business expo. The costs will vary depending on how many transactions, and whether the reports will be monthly or yearly. Both of these types of jobs can also be done by a relative or retired person looking for some extra income.

As for yourself, what is your time worth? – Evaluate your time and what it is truly worth to you, taking into account emotional, psychological as well as the financial considerations.

If you use filing or organizing as a means to take a break from a complex itinerary research, then do it. But if you find these tasks boring and your time could be spent more productively or producing income, it is time to look for outsourcing opportunities.

At this point in your business you have to trust that the old saying is true… "It takes money to make money" and paying for services will allow you to focus on what you do best, which is bringing in more clients, thus growing your business and *making more money.*

THE CUSTOMER COMES SECOND!

CEO Hal Rosenbluth chronicled the incredible success of his travel-services firm, Rosenbluth International, in his book, The Customer Comes Second.

Don't you love the title? Sometimes don't you wish it could be true? Well then, you may ask, "Who comes first"? The answer is elementary (my dear Watson). If you wish to really put your customers first, you must put your employees first more often.

I can hear you now. "But I don't have employees. I am a one-man (-woman) show. I seek out the leads, I go networking, I do the calls, I follow up, I make the sales, I file tax returns, and I send thank-you notes. I am the CEO, COO, Vice President of Sales, the CFO, the PR Director, the administrative assistant and the delivery boy all rolled into one. Heck, I even do Starbucks runs for the Boss (that would be you)." And we wonder why we, as home-based entrepreneurs, can become so cynical and stale.

The answer is simple. If you are the work force, you need to put YOURSELF first! If you burn out, if you crash, if you don't find the answer to the question, "What's the point of it all?" – there will be no customers in the first place, to put in the first place!

What if we put rebirth at the top of our agendas? As the marketplace becomes more and more demanding, the pace more and more relentless, it becomes especially important to bolster the renewal process. Here are some ideas on how to do that:

Take a serious daily break – Find the moment in the day where you can step aside and gather your thoughts. Planned coffee breaks are one thing, but I am talking about a serious "step aside and get collected" moment. I love to walk. I will set my things down and take a brisk walk around the golf course where I live. For you, it could be a mid-afternoon workout, meditation, jumping rope or taking a bubble bath. Spend time on yourself to be rejuvenated. (Extended Martini Lunches, however good they may be for client networking, are strongly discouraged for this purpose.)

Call time out – Turn off your cell phone and computer. Put the imaginary "closed" sign on your office and spend some time with the ones you love. Go to the movies with your kids, or send your kids to the movies and have a dinner with your loved one. Take an hour to read a book or catch up on reading the travel trade magazines. Call on a friend.

Have you considered relocating your office? – Get your calls forwarded to your cell phone. Take your lap top and find your local coffee shop. Sometimes, a change of scenery does wonders getting your life back in focus. All of a sudden, you will find clarity and order in the enormous task list as you sip your second Latte and breathe in the fresh air. As a matter of fact, as I am writing this book, I am in Mexico. I decided to practice what I preach and take a week off from my non-stop life to, not only take care of myself, but to reflect on where I have been and where I want to go with my business. But before I knew it, guilt crept in and I suddenly felt that I had to justify taking a whole week off. I started thinking, "too many obligations, too many responsibilities…how frivolous of me to consider taking a week off." I only gave myself permission once I justified the time off by promising myself to start this book that had been sitting on the back burner for a while. When I first arrived I was skeptical that I could make it through a full week staying by myself. I have now been here 5 days of the 7 day stay and I can honestly say that suddenly I am longing for a few more days. Already I am feeling rejuvenated and refreshed.

> *Take care of yourself in order to take care of your clients*

Do some spring cleaning – Get a paper shredder and start getting rid of all the paper and files you don't need. I sometimes take my stacks of papers and sort them in order of priority while watching TV. It's amazing how much you can accomplish during a 60-second commercial. There is great merit in inducing a feeling of order and creating a fresh start.

Attend a Seminar or a Travel related workshop – Go away for a bit. Meet other professionals in a fun, work environment. Make new friends and rub shoulders with the others in your business. Take a break and swap stories. It's fundamental to see what else is out there and what else is being done that works. Restructure your strategy and come back to a more productive work method.

Reward yourself – Do something that you consider rewarding. Corporations spend millions of dollars on perks and incentives to boost employee productivity. Spa treatments for your workforce (a.k.a. YOU) would be a well-justified expense. Get some fresh cut flowers. (Yes… even you men!!!).

Start smiling and caring – When I visit a coffee shop, I detest being made to feel like just another order. I don't know about you, but I like to receive a smile with my Latte. You owe your clients a smile during each phone call or meeting. Just try to be stressed or angry while smiling. It's impossible. Caring is an emotion and it cannot be delegated, nor can it be faked. Caring is what your customers want to see from you. If it shows that you take the time to take care of yourself, you will take the time to take care of them and that is why they will keep coming back to you.

DON'T BE A HOSTAGE IN YOUR HOME!

Ways you can avoid the "house arrest syndrome" while working at home

When working from home, we save on gas, dry cleaning, clothing and even contact lens solution. We don't have to commute or drive in bad weather conditions. But at times you may find yourself wishing that you had somewhere else to go besides the next room. And while it's really pretty mundane to most people, sometimes the simplest outings, such as a trip to the grocery store, can be a bit of an exciting event or a nice break in the day.

If you are at all extroverted, working from home is not always easy. During the winter, when everyone is moody and crabby anyway, the isolation factor can get magnified. Even if you are relatively introverted, you may find yourself wanting to spend more time with other people. Here are some ways you can do just that:

Take a Break! – At the end of the day when most people are ready to come home and relax, home-based agents can tire of looking at the surrounding four walls and are ready to get out. The problem for most of us is that it's hard to leave work alone. After all, the office is always there. "Maybe I'll check one more supplier." "Oh gosh, did I proof that last email?" It's hard to break away.

If you're longing for a break, I would suggest several possibilities. Take your laptop to a coffeehouse. Coffeehouses do seem to be the new mobile office and you can have fun while working there. They are places where you can meet other home-based business owners and strike up conversations and maybe get some business as a bonus. Another option is to regularly schedule lunches with friends or clients.

Who's the Boss? – All the sites promise that you can run a successful business from home without a boss, or at least not one looking over your shoulder all the time. Yet I've had great bosses before I took my business home – bosses who helped me grow, supported my ideas, highlighted my strong points, coached me on weak points, and gave me role models and opportunities. I replaced the traditional boss with "business buddies" or mentors who were willing to let me bounce ideas around and brainstorm with them. Remember, there will always be someone that you need to be accountable to. If you think a boss is difficult to please, wait until you're trying to please certain clients.

Make your work surroundings pleasant and conducive to being productive as possible.

Stay Disciplined! – Distractions are hard to resist. Could you throw in a load of laundry? Play with the kids? Call your mother? Stop at the grocery store? While we do have more flexibility than friends who are working 9 to 5, if we stop working to do something else we generally have to make up the time somehow, just as you would if you were working outside of the home in an office.

Although the benefits are numerous, the truth is, working from home can be overly romanticized. Work is work! Most people I know who work from home full-time and earn serious income know that running a business from home requires discipline and rules. If you brought your toddler to work, you couldn't spend your time chasing after her, could you? You're getting paid to perform services for a company. The same principle applies when you work from home. Any promise of "no child care" is not very realistic, unless you're able to stagger your hours.

Be Patient! – It's been almost 20 years since I started working from home. Along the way I've continued to develop self-discipline and worked on gaining clientele, and every day I challenge myself to learn something new.

Post Bail! – Posting bail means securing the release of someone (yourself) by providing security. You're not limited by hourly pay when you work at home. That means more money in your pocket if you're willing to put in the extra hours to get the work done. But you have to show collateral and make a concerted effort to grow.

Rehabilitate! – To rehabilitate means to restore to good health or useful life, as through therapy. Make your work surroundings pleasant and conducive to being as productive as possible. For example, my desk faces out to a large window. When the weather is nice, I sometimes work on my patio.

Working at home is hard work! – But by taking good care of yourself, disciplining your business and creating rules that you can live by, you will be paroled from the "House Arrest Syndrome" and released from that feeling that you're in jail. Set yourself free!

Chapter 4 | HOST AGENCIES

Database management programs, travel promoter laws, lead generation, supplier relationships, top commissions, overrides, training, mentoring programs are just a few considerations when operating a travel business. These systems and programs are all pre-established by a credible host agency. Aligning with this type of company means you can hit the ground running and start making money quickly.

HUNTING FOR A GOOD HOST AGENCY

There is a TV show that I occasionally watch called "House Hunters", which is a reality-style national television series about finding and purchasing a new home. The show takes viewers behind the scenes as individuals, couples and families learn what to look for and decide whether or not a home is meant for them.

By focusing on the "emotional experience" of finding and purchasing a new home, each episode shows the process as the buyers go through the search. You may experience the same emotions and decisions when looking for a good host agency.

COST – Many agents, especially those who are new to our industry, make a basic mistake. When deciding to get into the business of selling travel, they often make their more by emotion rather than logic. Many times I hear from a prospective affiliate "I want to get into this business because I'm passionate about travel." It's much less often that I hear someone say "I want to sell travel so that I can create a career and earn a living." Although passion is obviously a necessary component for success, if you buy on emotion only, you may end up "upside down" financially. To make an honest comparison of the host agencies on your list, you should consider all the costs you'll be facing. Just like buying real estate, you should take into

> *The investment you make with a good host agency should improve the quality and increase your overall equity*

consideration items such as start-up fees (down payment), monthly maintenance costs, association fees, insurance, etc. Based on your own projected potential earnings, you will need to figure out how much travel you must book before your total outlay will be recovered.

WEIGH THE PRICE – A host agency can actually save you money. I recommend that you create a worksheet and list all of the costs of running the business on your own versus aligning with a host agency. Factor in the costs of bookkeeping, back-office support, seller of travel requirements, technology, E&O insurance, database management services, etc. Many of these expenses are covered when you sign with a host agency.

SIZE – Just like the size of a new house, you have to look at the size of your host agency. The size of your host agency is important to your bottom line, since commission splits are (or should be) based on the percentage amount that a host agency earns from the supplier. For example, if your agreement says that you will earn 75% commission, you will want to make sure that you are paid that split from whatever the agency is earning. When you sign with a host agency, consider all of the features it offers but also find out about the commission structure. Large-volume host agencies earn commissions at the top-level tiers.

FEATURES – There are a whole "host" of benefits that most of the reputable host agencies offer. Consider asking the following questions: Is there some type of ongoing training? Does the host have staff dedicated just to the needs and training of someone new to the industry? Does the host have a mentoring program? What does the agency offer seasoned or experienced agents? Do they already work with successful agents? What type of overall support is available? Is there an agent-to-agent information exchange? Is someone available only during normal business hours or 24 Hours a day? Do you have direct access to the owner or manager?

CLIENT'S LIFESTYLE – Take into consideration your client database when doing your search. Are your clients mostly leisure, corporate, honeymooners or families? If your clients are mainly leisure, maybe a GDS system isn't necessary for your business.

LOCATION – Does it really matter now that almost everything has gone electronic? It's more important to find an agency that gives you that "neighborly" feel. Does the host "pick up your mail" while you are gone? In other words, do they take care of your business and clients while you are away?

ASSOCIATIONS – Make sure your host agency is in good standing with most of the top associations in the industry that are geared to the needs of home-based agents and host agencies, namely OSSN, ASTA, and PATH. PATH (Professional Association of Travel Hosts) is an excellent resource for agents looking for a credible host as they require their members to go through a rigorous business and personal background check. Host agencies must adhere to a strict code of ethics and are only admitted to PATH if they qualify under the membership requirements.

(www.PATH4Hosts.com)

Check credentials and referrals.

- Make sure that there are no unresolved formal complaints or lawsuits against the agency or owner
- Stay away from agencies that have "travel agent recruiting" programs and tout offering travel discounts by offering ID cards.

The investment you make in a good host agency should improve the quality of your business life while living there and increase your overall equity. Just like the participants in the TV show, if you do your research well, you will eventually find the perfect home!

Chapter 5 | TRAVEL CONFERENCE

THE POINT OF THE MEETING – HOW YOU CAN MAKE THE MOST OUT OF ATTENDING A TRAVEL AGENT CONFERENCE

Conferences can be expensive gatherings that overwhelm attendees with new information, chances for networking and demonstrations of business tools. While scheduling effectively and paying close attention is key, it's your preparation before you even attend that can make a big difference.

Hallway conversations can be a valuable source of information-sharing during conferences.

Because traveling to the conference site can be expensive, it's important to choose the show that makes the most sense for your business goals. Obviously, if you're a home-based agent, conferences such as the Home-Based Travel Agent Forum are more geared toward specific, pertinent issues. But there are also shows put on by consortia, such as Vacation.com, and other industry associations.

Here are some tips for getting the most out of your conference attendance:

Be prepared and know the facts – Determine the total cost to attend, including registration, hotel, airfare, ground transportation and meals. There are always time-sensitive cost savings when the show is initially announced. Securing the best deals early on, such as early-bird registration and discounted hotel rates, will help you avoid the surprising high costs later.

Stay at the conference hotel – If you want to maximize your chances to socialize, staying at the conference hotel can be a plus. You also will save time and taxi costs.

Pack light so you can bring material home – You will need that extra space in your luggage to bring all the brochures home. With the extra baggage fees from the airlines, it may be less expensive to ship the material home from the hotel business center.

Have a plan before you go to the show – Take a look at the conference website, the different tracks and the speakers, and then figure out how your time can be spent most effectively. Make sure you schedule your time around sessions you don't want to miss. Before the conference begins, sit down with the printable version of the program and go through the agenda with a highlighter and mark anything that looks interesting.

Wear comfortable but professional business attire – These are "business" conferences after all, and you should dress accordingly. Don't forget good shoes, since you will be walking a lot.

Make the most of the tradeshow floor – The tradeshow floor is a great opportunity to meet a multitude of suppliers and high-level executives. They will be eager for you to learn more about their products and how they may fit your clients' needs. Take the time to introduce yourself to those staffing the different booths.

Bring plenty of business cards – It's awkward when you reach into your wallet or purse to discover you're out of cards.

Don't focus on your laptop or cell phone – I've been at many conferences where most of the audience is looking down at their laptops or cell phones. Are they taking notes? Or is everyone just catching up on emails and texting? If so, they may be missing the valuable information being presented. Be in the moment. We spend too much of our time staying distracted. Turn off your cell phone, your Blackberry or iPhone, as well as computer. Laptops and texting can also sometimes be very distracting to the speaker and your seatmates. Try to keep typing to a minimum during sessions or sit in an area off to the side of the room if you must use your laptop. Check the program with the show management since session content may be available online after the show.

Use the conference to network with your peers – Hallway conversations can be a valuable source of information-sharing during conferences. Try not to sit with the same people you came with. Later you will have time to go to dinner and reconnect. Arrive early to the session so you can introduce yourself to anyone sitting next to you. Instead of waiting for them to speak with you, take the first step. Before you leave the conference, sit down and write out a minimum of two things you plan to change when you get back to your business and why.

Conferences are a great use of your time, especially if you leave with new ideas fostered by some great speaker on how to change and grow. For each individual session that you attend, try to take away a minimum of three good points from each of the presentations. Your goal should be to increase your knowledge.

Chapter 6 | HARNESSING YOUR EXPERTISE

Give your clients the benefit of your travel knowledge

You have taken all of the CLIA courses, satisfied all of the ship inspections, sailed on all of the required cruises and finally earned your ACC (Accredited Cruise Counselor), MCC (Master Cruise Counselor) or even ECC (Elite Cruise Counselor). Or maybe you have enrolled in The Travel Institute's training and certification programs and have become a CTA (Certified Travel Associate) or CTC (Certified Travel Counselor). Have you become a destination specialist? If so, you have traveled to the destination to experience it first hand and you have taken the required courses to be certified. If you have completed any if these types of training programs, good for you!

The Travel Institute says that these types of credentials give you the knowledge, confidence and status that set you apart as a true travel professional. CLIA says that their certification programs are prestigious and will provide you a business advantage by increasing your cruise knowledge and, in turn, your client's confidence in you. Both of these statements are absolutely true since any agent will certainly benefit from their excellent training and certification programs.

> *Get the word out! You've taken then training and have the designation – now promote your expertise*

The main reason you would want to enroll in these types of programs is to become a more knowledgeable travel consultant and ultimately grow your business. But how well are you using such trainings and certifications as a marketing tool? I have seen agents that have been fiercely focused on getting their accreditations and designations, and they have all the initials behind their names to prove it. Now it's time to let everyone know about your accomplishments. Here are a few ways to get the word out so that you can get best payback for the time and money you've invested.

ANNOUNCE THE DESIGNATION

Not only announce your new accreditation to your database but also let your clients know exactly what the designation stands for. Make sure that in your newsletter you spell out the actual designation, such as CLIA's ACC - Accredited Cruise Counselor. Start off by saying something like "I am proud to announce….. Completing this rigorous training program will add to the service and expertise that I can provide when planning your next vacation."

IN YOUR SIGNATURE – Incorporate all of your accreditations and niche specialties as part of your signature on any correspondence, including emails. A home-based agent that I know uses the title of "Personal Travel Consultant". On the second line she has "Italy Destination Specialist" and on the third line she lists "Certified Rail Europe Agent". Another agent adds a line after her name and designation that says, "CTC - Certified Travel Counselor – The Travel Institute's Prestigious Certification Program."

ON YOUR BUSINESS CARD – Since there isn't a lot of room on a small business card, I have seen many agents use fold over business cards, creating a mini brochure or even using the back of a card to carry the information.

SEND PRESS RELEASES TO YOUR LOCAL NEWSPAPER – Title it something like: "Local travel consultant completes the rigorous training offered by The Travel Institute and earns the prestigious status of CTA (Certified Travel Associate). The Travel Institute states that **Certified Travel Professionals** provide in-depth destination knowledge, industry experience, and top-notch customer service. Members of The Travel Institute provide a personal link to cruise lines, airlines, car rental companies, hotels, and tour companies to ensure your satisfaction."

This can be especially newsworthy if you have become a "Lifestyle Specialist" such as Accessible Travel, Adventure Travel, Gay and Lesbian Travel, Golf, etc. I know of an agent who an Accessible Travel Specialist who also happens to be blind. She sent out a press release about becoming a specialist and also mentioned that she was escorting a group of blind people and called it "The Blind Leading the Blind Cruise." The story was first picked up by a local paper and then a national newspaper, and then eventually it was also syndicated because it was considered newsworthy and interesting. What started out as a press release about her being an Accessible Travel Specialist ultimately became the best advertising possible for her business.

"Unless it says Ph.D. after your name, the general public is not likely to know what the initials stand for or what it took for you to get them."

ADD THE DESIGNATION TO YOUR WEBSITE, FACEBOOK, TWITTER AND OTHER SOCIAL MEDIA – Here's where you are not limited by space or cost requirements and you can really go into more detail about the accreditations. Make it look like an official notice and use the same format as for a press release. Start with a date and then add "For Immediate Release – Press Release" and insert the announcement.

Remember, unless it says Ph.D. after your name, the general public is not likely to know what the initials stand for or what it took to get them. Until you enlighten your audience this information is only exciting to you.

CREATE TRAVEL GUIDES

All of us who travel have had disasters that make us smarter travelers "the next time." But how many of us are turning these bad experiences into tips or suggestions to pass along to our clients? I'm not suggesting merely verbal communication but actually putting it in writing and creating tips sheets and guides.

As an example, the first time I went to Europe I soon found out that the travel there was quite different than in the United States – from electrical connections to language barriers to currency conversion. I distinctly remember the panic I felt when a hotel in Italy asked for my passport and told me that they would be keeping it until I checked out. I protested quite vocally and they looked at me like "here's another crazy American." I had no idea that this was common in many hotels in foreign countries. The only advice I had previously received about passports was "whatever you do, don't lose it."

While traveling over the years, I have said to myself many times, "If I only knew." I then realized that preparing clients for cultural differences up front will assure minimal disappointment.

Here are some tips that I give my clients who are touring out of the country for the first time:

Carry your passport with you at all times or lock it up in the hotel safe to ensure against loss or theft. For added protection, keep a photocopy of your passport with you and another one in your suitcase. Before you leave home, please send another copy to me. Be sure to take my phone number with you so that if you lose your passport I can fax you a copy. Note: Don't be alarmed if the hotel asks for your passport. Hotels are sometimes required to hold your passport overnight to comply with local regulations. You should ask when you can expect it to be returned.

Europe's hospitality industry is centuries old and its hotels often reflect the varied traditions and standards of their respective countries. While these accommodations are comfortable, be prepared for differences and don't expect European hotels to be the same as those at home. Rooms in European hotels are often smaller than in U.S. hotels. Also, when booking a triple room, the third bed may be a rollaway cot.

> *"Start creating your own travel guides just by using your own personal experiences."*

Here are some other tips to offer your tour clients:

- The tour company will usually arrange for wake-up calls for all passengers depending on the agenda for the following day. Should the call not go through, or if you are a heavy sleeper and don't hear it, your own back-up alarm clock is good insurance.

- It's important to be considerate of others on the tour and to be prompt at meeting times and places. Make sure you know where and when to meet the group in the morning.

- It's a good idea to ask your tour director for his or her room number in case it's needed for any reason.

- Rather than bringing one umbrella to share, it's better for everyone to have his or her own fold-up umbrella. If it rains during mild weather, this will eliminate the need to carry a raincoat while touring.

- You will not be allowed in most churches and cathedrals if you are wearing shorts, sleeveless blouses or short-sleeved shirts.

- Washcloths are not standard in most hotels in Europe. Take towelettes or cut an old bath towel from home into squares to use as washcloths. When you are done with them, just throw them away.

- When sightseeing on your own, remember to take a business card from the hotel. Should the taxi cab driver not speak English, you can show him the card.

- If you like to shop, remember to take into consideration airline weight restrictions and pack lightly or take an extra suitcase to allow for purchases.

Start creating your own travel guides just by using your personal experiences. Take a journal with you on every trip and write down notes when you experience something that you think would be helpful for your clients. It's also a good habit to listen to fellow travelers to hear what they think, both good and bad.

You can promote your business by putting your travel tips in a letter or set of documents that you personalize just for your clients. Send the tips to them by email or include a printed sheet with their documents. Your suggestions and tips to make your clients' vacation more carefree will be appreciated and remembered long after the bottle of wine has been drunk, the flowers have died or the welcome home note has been put in the trash.

TURN FIRST-TIME CRUISERS INTO LIFE-TIME CRUISERS

Do you remember your first cruise? I can remember mine like it was yesterday. It was about the time of the popular TV series "The Love Boat". I would watch that show week after week and visualized all of the wonderful experiences I could have on a cruise. I would spend hours reading through those beautiful brochures and dreaming. I planned and saved, and the time finally came. I was so excited! The journey, however, did not begin the way I expected.

Arriving at the pier, I was directed to give my luggage to the porters, whom I found to be very abrupt, to the point of downright rudeness. After leaving my bags, I started worrying because the porters made me feel that the tip that I left was not adequate and I was now certain that I would never see my bags on board the ship.

Being a novice cruiser, I found the check-in process to be very confusing and the whole embarkation process quite chaotic and nerve-wracking. After taking quite some time to get to the front of the line, I was informed that I was missing additional immigration forms. The annoyed cruise line representative pointed out that I should have picked these forms up at the table in the entrance area.

Give your clients as complete a picture as possible of what cruising is all about.

After filling out the additional forms, getting back in line, receiving my boarding card, I was finally ready to get on board. However, going up the gangplank it seems I can't get onboard until my picture is taken. So now I am thinking "Do I have to pay for this? What if I don't like it?" and in a decision that I later regretted, I refused the picture opportunity. One more security scan, and at last I am standing in the atrium of the ship and I am truly in awe. I finally recognize some of the visions that were painted in my mind by those wonderful brochures. Hold on though…there was more! All of a sudden a lot of foreign jargon was thrown at me. I was informed that no "stewards" were available to

take me to my "stateroom". A nice young man looked at my boarding card and told me to go past the "purser's desk," take the elevator up to the "Empress Deck," then go "aft" and my stateroom would be on the "starboard" side.

Whew…a half an hour later and I finally made it to the room. Time to start my vacation, right? Not quite! Wait...what's that announcement? Mandatory emergency evacuation drill? Life vests? Following the hordes of other cruisers, there we were lined up like dutiful soldiers in our bright day-glow orange vests. Everyone stood in the open deck with our "Love Boat" make-up and hair do's melting in the heat and humidity of a mid-summer day in Florida. How did I miss reading about this lovely experience in the brochure?

Ah, and then there was my luggage. My premonition about that angry porter almost came true, as my first bag arrived just as the ship was leaving and the final bag getting to me around 11:00PM. Not the best way to start off a long anticipated vacation.

Don't get me wrong. Cruising is still my favorite way to travel, and it was this particular cruise that led me to the travel business.

Most occurrences we have no control over, but if a traveler is prepared for what to expect in advance, it makes traveling all the more enjoyable. I vowed that once I became a travel agent, I would give my clients as complete a picture as possible of what cruising was all about.

This led me to write personalized guides, using my own mishaps and adventures to describe what to avoid and what not to miss. Even though the suppliers do a good job of including these types of details with the documents, most people do not read through the reams and reams of information that is provided, and by the time they get they receive their documents, it is too late to prepare properly.

Clients will take notice of anything that is personalized and applies to their particular trip. I try to send out my "First Time Cruiser Guide" as soon as a deposit is made, so that my clients can better prepare. An even better scenario would be to sit down with clients and personally go over the tips and information. If distance or timing doesn't allow this, I send them a guide and follow with an offer to go through the details with them and answer any questions by phone.

Don't forget to include information on the all-important proof-of-citizenship requirements, information on how the cashless system works on board, tipping guidelines, what to pack, basic cruise lingo, address concerns about motion sickness (but do not to give medical advice), and how to prepare for the last night of the cruise, such as, gratuity envelopes and protocol, putting suitcases out before going to bed and keeping only personal items, medicine and something to wear for the next day, etc. Tell them to avoid the long lines at the Purser's desk by not waiting until the last night to check or pay their final bill. Also, don't forget to let them know about customs procedures before getting off the ship, and how and where to claim luggage.

It's also important to tell clients that even though the ship arrives at 8AM, that doesn't mean they will disembark at 8AM. I let my clients know that it can take some time, so go have a leisurely breakfast, bring a book or magazine and find a lovely place to relax until you are called. The first and last day is where you will often see the tempers fly and nerves frazzle, mainly because passengers aren't prepared for what to expect.

You want clients to have a great experience from beginning to end so, they will come back and book cruises year after year. There is nothing worse than to be on a cruise hearing upset passengers say "my travel agent never told me!"

ANSWERING THE CRUISING "WHAT IF'S"

Providing a Smooth Cruise Experience

Getting onboard a ship it is easy to notice those passengers who are experiencing cruising for the first time. Just getting off of a cruise myself, I first noticed the gentleman who walked around the entire cruise with his video camera glued to his right eye, even while in his tuxedo on formal night. Then there was the woman who smiled and thanked the bartender who offered her the fancy drink with the umbrella on it. I watched as she almost choked with embarrassment as she swallowed her first sip when he asked for her boarding card for the charge. Or on the opposite end, I saw a family run past the embarkation photo opportunity when they thought that they might be charged.

> *"If the traveler knows what to expect, it makes traveling all the more enjoyable."*

If we don't share our expertise, clients may be disappointed or miss out in the overall cruise experience.

What if the client booked their own air incorrectly? Your clients tell you that they already booked their air and now they want you to take care of the cruise. Great! But then you find out that the air arrangements they made are all wrong.

When leaving for a cruise always tell clients to plan to arrive by noon – at the latest – on embarkation day. The day before is even better. The reason: You need to factor in possible flight delays and other transportation glitches that could keep them from getting to the pier on time.

Your clients booked a 9:30AM return flight home because the cruise arrived at 7:00AM and thought that would give them plenty of time … wrong! If they can't change the flight to noon or later, tell them to advise the purser's office about their flight time so that arrangements can be made for priority early disembarkation. (Then wish them luck!) There are too many variables, such as, delays with customs, traffic, etc., that could prevent them from possibly making their flight home.

What if my luggage doesn't show up at the airport? You will never understand how unsettling this can be unless it happens to you. And if you travel much, sooner or later, it will. Tell your clients that carry-ons are key. Pack everything needed to get them through dinnertime – and possibly the next day – including bathing suits, cameras, medications, a change of clothes and toiletries. Once on board, it is important to go immediately to the purser's desk and tell them about the situation. They deal with this on every cruise and have procedures for assisting guests, including providing "care packages" that include toiletries, tee shirts, etc. Having assisted many clients through this ordeal I am always amazed when luggage shows up one or two ports later.

What if I get sea-sick? Remember, you are not a doctor, so do not dispense medical advice. You might want to tell them that sea-sickness is highly unlikely but they should talk to their doctor for recommendations based on their own health history. Many passengers anticipate motion sickness and take medication before they even get on board and end up having a bad reaction or sleepiness when they most likely will forget that they are at sea because it is so calm and smooth. I try to describe the modern ship stabilizers and equate them to the shock absorbers on a luxury vehicle, such as a Mercedes. Clients will find it reassuring that should they feel ill, motion sickness medication is available in the gift shops or in the infirmary on board.

What if I miss the ship? People get left behind in ports all the time. It's the client's responsibility to be back on time or find their own way, at their expense, to the next port. Advise to always take identification, credit cards or enough funds on shore to get to the next port. If they are nervous about this possibility tell them to consider taking shore excursions offered by the cruise line. If one of the ship's organized tours is late, they will definitely hold the ship until the tour gets back.

What if I forget to keep cash at the end of the cruise to pay the tips? Cash is no longer always needed. As I learned on my last cruise, some cruise lines automatically charge the gratuities to the bill at the end of the cruise. It is best to find out in advance what are the cruise line's current policies are regarding gratuities.

The next time you are on a cruise and you really want to learn what clients need help with, stand by the purser's desk and listen to the strange questions from passengers. Then you will truly understand where the joke "Do you know what time the midnight buffet is?" came from.

IT'S ALL ABOUT THE KIDS!

Help your clients turn traveling with children into Child's Play…

While travel is fun, family vacations can be challenging, stressful, with long stretches of boredom and days of over-stimulation. Providing tips will reduce the stress and increase the enjoyment of your client's vacation. I turned my own experiences, and those of my clients, into a guide that I provided for all who would be traveling with children. Here are some excerpts from that guide.

- Instead of listening to lots of "buy me this, buy me that" routines when you travel, tell kids how much you will give them for souvenirs at each destination, and then they get to decide how to spend their money.
- Upon arrival after flying, purchase a small Styrofoam cooler before going to the hotel. Most hotels, campgrounds, etc. have ice available – often for free. Purchase groceries

in a local store. Refrigerated items may be stored in the small cooler, even on the road.

- When traveling with children, purchase postcards from your vacation destinations, let them write on the back about their thoughts and experiences. Punch a hole in the top corner and assemble them onto an expandable ring. You will have an enjoyable time reflecting back on past vacations experienced during childhood years.
- When traveling with children ALWAYS carry a current photo of each child. This will prove invaluable if you accidentally get separated.
- If you are in a crowded place or attraction, arrange for a meeting place in case you get separated.
- When flying with small children, carry on a plastic, restaurant drink cup with a lid and a straw. The flight attendant will gladly fill up your child's cup for you. This is a comfortable way to avoid spills.
- With older children walkie-talkies can be invaluable for keeping track of everyone in busy tourist areas. Look for the ones with the widest range. Kids will have fun using them as well.
- Make a sleeping bag style roll of each of your children's daily vacation outfits with the socks, shirt, etc. secured with a rubber band. You won't believe how much easier it is for them to find their outfit each morning. They can pull out their rubber-banded outfit with all the pieces together. Even the little ones can get it out of the suitcase and put their clothes on unattended. No more, "Mommy, I can't find my socks!"
- Parents taking children on extended trips or abroad should make an appointment with the pediatrician well in advance to be sure their children get pre-travel check-ups and are up to date with all childhood vaccinations.
- Bring along plenty of your children's favorite foods, and snacks for long flights as well as reading material, games and other activities they enjoy. A 24-hour supply of food is recommended for infants and toddlers in case of major delays.
- Children often experience earaches as a result of changes in air pressure during flights, especially during take-off and descent. Bring chewing gum and encourage

them to yawn, chew and swallow. Children flying with even a mild cold should take an over-the-counter children's decongestant prior to takeoff and landing.

- Pack all important medications and those that might be needed during flight (prescription drugs, allergy medications, Tylenol, etc.) in a carry-on bag.
- Make sure older children know the address and telephone number of where you are staying and all other emergency information. Give younger children a card with the same information.
- In hot climates make sure children wear hats and other protective clothing, drink plenty of fluids and regularly apply sunscreen with at least SPF30.
- There are special preparations of insect repellents made specifically for children. In the areas where the risk of mosquito bites is high, it is important to apply the sunscreen first and the insect repellent next, as the vapors from the insect repellent are necessary in order for them to work.

I always make a "Travel Kit for Kids" to give to my clients with their documents. Dollar stores are a great resource where you can find everything from card games like "Go Fish", coloring books, beach balls, swim goggles and much more. You can also include a box of raisins, chewing gum or other healthy snacks. The kids love digging in the bags and finding things they can use throughout their trip. Parents love it when you include something that is fun as well as educational. As an example, I found a children's book on dolphins that I gave to a family that was going to experience swimming with the dolphins in Mexico.

Providing fun kid's travel kits and tips for your traveling families will lessen the calls of "Are we there yet?"

Chapter 7 | STEPS TO SUCCESS

FROM IMAGINATION TO REALITY

I still find it hard to believe that I actually used visualization exercises to find the house I currently live in. This is a technique that did not come easy to me and was something I had to learn through instructional goal-setting sessions.

During my initial session I had expressed a desire to move. When the trainer asked me to give him more details about my new house, I was vague. At that particular point, all I knew was that I wanted to downsize to a condominium or townhouse. He then made me painstakingly describe **exactly** what my new house would look like by asking me a long series of questions, such as what color are the walls, how many stories, does it have fireplace, what does each room look like and what views does the house have.

How to find success in selling travel by visualizing the result you want.

I followed the instructions to write down all of the attributes I had described, and then I looked at the list several times a day. It wasn't very long after that a friend took me to see some condos in a part of town that I was unfamiliar with. There it was - my house, exactly as I visualized it…down to every detail!

I have since tried to incorporate this same technique into my travel business. One recent example was when I organized a marketing and planning retreat for some of my agents. We went away for a 2-night stay in Monterey, California to strategize about upcoming opportunities, brainstorm new marketing ideas and set annual goals.

> *"You need to prepare yourself to act and be successful, and visualizing success will help you do just that."*

In preparation for the getaway I requested that all my agents bring some of their favorite magazines for a special project. I purchased framed cork boards for each of us and brought along all of my scrapbook-making supplies. The conference room soon started looking like a craft store as the puzzled agents tried to figure out what in the world we were about to do.

I asked everyone to start going through all of the magazines and cut out any pictures, quotes, words or anything else that might represent what they wanted to achieve for the coming year. Just as I was instructed to do when visualizing my house, I asked each of them to be very specific with what they wanted to see materialize.

I also cautioned everyone as they started to work on the project to be careful what they wished for. For example, when it comes to earning more money don't put a picture of a one dollar bill on the board unless you only want to earn a dollar. If you are going to visualize success, dream big. Find a picture of the denomination of money that you truly would love to be earning. If earning enough in commissions to buy a new car is important, make sure your picture is of the exact make and model of the car that you want.

There were lots of words being cut out like “SUCCESS”, “FINANCIAL FREEDOM”, “ORGANIZE”, “DREAM” and my personal favorite, “BELIEVE”. Next to travel scenes they pasted pictures of money representing increased commissions. Several wanted to increase their group business, so they found pictures of groups traveling on tours and cruises. A couple of the agents had family pictures and others had lifestyle pictures.

One agent expressed that her goal was to learn how to balance here family life with her travel business. In each case these pictures and sayings represented something that was pertinent to achieving their success. It was fascinating to see how each project was completely unique as each agent explained what the board meant to them.

Does this all sound hokey to you? Consider the fact that I am not the only one who uses these powerful techniques. There are winning football coaches who have given their players pictures of Super Bowl rings before the season begins. Golf superstar Tiger Woods incorporates visualization into his pre-swing routine. The Los Angeles Lakers coach asks his players to visualize victory before games. And Olympic swimmers have used visualization and relaxation techniques before races.

I remember a scene in the movie “American Beauty” where Annette Benning, playing a realtor, is getting a house ready to view. She can be seen vacuuming and opening drapes while chanting, "I WILL sell this house" over and over. This scene reinforces my belief that it isn't just a matter of preparing business plans and financial reports, you also need to prepare yourself to act and be successful, and visualizing success will help you do just that.

STEPS TO SUCCESS

To be successful requires effort and energy – Not only must you actively recruit new clients; you must stay on top of them to ensure that they maintain a loyal business relationship with you. Remember, having loyal, repeat clients is the way to make money in this industry.

So understand going in that this is a business that will require real effort on your part and a sustained effort at that. But what in life that's worthwhile doesn't, right?

Have a plan to keep yourself motivated – No longer will there be a boss looking over your shoulder, so from now on, motivating yourself is YOUR job. If setting goals helps you motivate, then you should also reward yourself when those goals are met. Because you're earning commissions on sales generated by you, you will continue to make an income as long as you work hard – that's enough motivation in itself.

Financial Commitment – Financially, a home-based travel business generally has relatively low set-up costs compared to other small business/franchise start-ups. Allow a budget for ongoing marketing expenses, office equipment purchases, maintenance and repairs.

Who is best suited? – It should be obvious from what has been said above that in order to be successful working your travel business from home that you have to be someone who's a self-starter and is able to persuade others to buy from you. If, on the other hand, you're someone who needs someone else to poke you into action when it comes to work or business, being independent is probably not for you.

Of course, if you're going to take on this role, you will need to be comfortable dealing with people. This doesn't always mean face to face, of course. If you're running your business on the Internet, you will probably never meet a lot of those clients. But you still must be able to communicate effectively. Common sense suggests that the more outgoing and sociable you are, the more you are going to enjoy this sort of role and the better you will be at it as a result. If you're more of a recluse than a social butterfly, it's unlikely you're going to be able to comfortably get out there and do what has to be done to keep your business on track.

Selling travel is a very personal way of selling. You must exercise your own powers of persuasion and influence to encourage others to buy from you. It is imperative, therefore, that you are 100% behind the products, destinations and suppliers that you are promoting. Do NOT lend your name or endorsement to something that you are not genuinely committed to selling.

Look at your job like a top chef who includes all the right ingredients

As someone who enjoys cooking and entertaining, I have to admit that I am hooked on some of television's competition cooking shows. Recently, while watching an episode of "Top Chef" I couldn't help but compare the challenges we face as travel agents with those of the competing chefs.

"Top Chef" is a show in which chefs compete against each other in weekly challenges. They are judged by a panel of professional chefs, and one or more contestants are eliminated from the competition each week. Each episode has two challenges, the Quickfire Challenge and the Elimination Challenge. In the first, each chef is asked to cook a dish with certain requirements, for example, using specific ingredients or to inspire a certain taste. They are usually given an hour or less to complete these tasks.

So here's my home-based agent's Quickfire Challenge: Just as a recipe will fail without all of the proper ingredients, so will your sales effort. When beginning the process of working with a new client, it is crucial not to miss one "ingredient" or misinterpret what our clients ask for. Doing so will surely result in being eliminated from the competition.

The first contact with a client is usually a "Quickfire" or brief overview of what they are looking for in a vacation. It is critical in these first stages of communication to listen carefully and intently. At the same time that you qualify your credentials, it is helpful to repeat back to the client what you think you heard. For example, "Thank you for giving me the opportunity to plan your Hawaii vacation. By the way, I am a Hawaii Destination Specialist and have traveled there many times myself. After I find the perfect package for you, I would be happy provide you with recommendations for tours, dining and other activities. But before I take down your contact information, I would like to recap what you are looking for. Your preferred airport is San Francisco, there will be 2 adults and 2 children traveling and it's important that you have a non-smoking room. Would you like a room with a full ocean view? You also mentioned that you would like a car. Would you like a full-size or convertible?"

In the "Top Chef" Elimination Challenge, the chefs have to prepare one or more dishes to meet the challenge requirements and some may require several courses. For agents, that may mean several destinations. The chefs *(and agents)* may have from a few hours to a few days to complete this challenge. If specified by the challenge, the chefs *(and agents)* are given a limited budget to shop at a specific store *(read "travel supplier" for the agents)* to complete their task.

At the end of the challenge, the chefs wait to be brought to the Judges' *(Your client's)* table, where the judges deliberate on the best and worst dishes *(package/pricing)*. One individual is named the "Top Chef" for the challenge and one chef is determined to be the worst, and they are asked to "pack his knives and go."

What's intriguing about the concept of Top Chef is how in one episode a chef can win a challenge and then in the next episode make one small mistake and be totally eliminated from the show. Just as in "Top Chef", travel agents' service and past performance are only as good as our next opportunity.

I distinctly remember an incident which almost cost me a very lucrative client. Just as with their past trips, I thought I had done everything right. I gave them a beautiful going-away basket, arranged for a private limo to take them to the airport and I sent the VIP letters to the hotels. But I forgot to verify that they had seat assignments on their flights that the cruise line had arranged. My client was furious when she returned and I almost lost all future business from this client because I missed that one vital "ingredient" to make their trip a total success. To avoid having this happen again, I use an extensive checklist for every reservation

The Final Challenge: Agents are constrained by budgets and how well we can interpret all of the information provided. We submit our quotes knowing that the client is comparing all the elements against our competition. But it is important to remember that in many cases we are awarded the sale not only because of pricing, but other factors such as expertise, helpfulness, and good salesmanship. Once you have all of these main ingredients just right, rather than asking you to "pack your knives and leave" you will be awarded the sale, which will be the "frosting on the cake."

"Our challenge is how well we can interpret all of the information provided."

GROW YOUR BUSINESS BY CONFRONTING YOUR FEARS

What's preventing you from being successful? Are you feeling stuck? Do you allow others to define your potential? You can't break through to your next level of success unless you understand what's holding you back. The "Fs" in life can get in the way or help you grow your business. Here are some to consider.

Fear – To be successful in business, you must step outside your comfort zone and move through the fear. Many times I've come up with what I thought was a great idea, but then stopped short of executing it when I started to doubt myself. I can remember one specific time when I decided to approach some other businesses to see if they would be interested in co-marketing. I reflected on my fears and thought "What if they reject my idea?" But I pushed through those doubts and ended up with positive results with a large majority of those businesses.

Frustration – Not being able to get clients to return your calls or emails can be frustrating, especially when you've done all the work and now have a limited time to hold the reservation. Whatever the circumstances are, don't give up until you feel that you've exhausted all avenues. Then don't dwell on it, move on.

Failure – We're conditioned to avoid failure at all costs. We operate within safe boundaries where success is most assured and shirk off "difficult" tasks because of our fear of failure. I have a note posted on my computer that says, "Rejection means nothing to me." Each time a customer tells me "no," I look at the sentence and try again. I look at my failures as opportunities to improve. I ask myself, what could I do differently the next time? What lesson did I learn? As the old saying goes "try, try again." In sales, of course, it's a numbers game. The more times you try, the more chances there are for success.

Faulty assumptions – Eliminate self-created barriers to your success and focus on the facts. Don't just assume that because a client didn't book a trip with you this time that you did something wrong. There could have been a myriad of personal reasons why he or she chose not to go with you. Instead, proceed on the assumption that the client will indeed use your services in the future. Thank him or her for giving you the opportunity, and then let it be known that you hope to be able to be of service the next time.

NOW CONSIDER THESE POSITIVE "F's"

Focus on the possibilities – Accept the challenge of finding new business, clients and opportunities. This means getting out there and always trying something new. It can be pretty scary but also very exciting to imagine what can open up next.

Fearlessness – Getting unstuck requires taking action and courage. Contact that customer who rejected your last quote. Schedule a meeting with the Pied Piper for whom you think you have found the perfect group trip. Take on that project that you've been thinking about for the last two years. Get yourself a "can do" attitude.

Fortune – Fortune is out there waiting for you to claim it. Here's a poem taken from my first book, "How I Made a Small Fortune as a Home-Based Travel Agent." I often look at this when I hesitate to do something that's out of my comfort zone.

STEP OUT OF THE COMFORT ZONE

I used to have a comfort zone where I knew I couldn't fail,
The same four walls and busywork were really more like jail,
I longed so much to do the things I'd never done before,
But stayed inside my comfort zone and paced the same old floor.
I said it didn't matter that I wasn't doing much,
I said I didn't care for things like commission checks and such,
I claimed to be so busy with the things inside my zone,
But deep inside I longed for that special success of my own.
I couldn't let my life go by just
Watching others win.
I held my breath—I stepped outside
And let the change begin,
I took a step and with new strength
I'd never felt before.
I kissed my comfort zone good-bye

And closed and locked the door.

If you're in a comfort zone afraid to venture out,

Remember that all winners were at

one time filled with doubt.

A step or two and words of praise

Can make your dreams come true.

Reach for your future with a smile

Success is there for you!

Chapter 8 | WORKING WITH SUPPLIERS

GETTING R.E.S.P.E.C.T. FROM THE INDUSTRY

When I first started my home-based travel business in 1992, I was surprised at how the travel industry viewed "outside agents." It seemed that the consensus was that if you did not work in a traditional storefront agency, you were not legitimate or professional, and were only in it for the "travel perks."

One of the terms I heard whispered was that outside agents were "Kitchen Table Mable's." I also remember the time I attended an industry trade show and overheard suppliers complaining that only "Condo-Commandos" were attending the event. They were asking "Where are the *REAL* travel agents?"

Having been an independent contractor in the electronic industry, where my expertise and customer service skills were highly valued and appreciated, I certainly wasn't accustomed to this type of "cold shoulder."

How to be recognized by suppliers as a knowledgeable and talented travel professional

Well, I am pleased to say, we have come a long way, baby! Suppliers have now recognized the selling power of the professional home-based agent. In a survey of average travel industry salaries based on job titles, independent contractors came in second, after owners, with earning power.

Even with all of this new-found recognition and attention, however, there are still some remnants of hesitancy to work with home-based agents on the part of the district sales managers (DSMs). First, you need to recognize their position before you can get their attention and support. DSMs are compensated based on sales growth performance and meeting their goals and projections. Therefore, it is prudent on your part to be the one aggressively pursuing the supplier relationship.

Don't forget, because you are in a home location, most of you are hard to find. It's not easy for suppliers to come knocking at your door when they don't know where your door is. That's why you will need to be proactive and take the steps to get their attention.

Here are some of the steps that I have taken to establish good working relationships, thereby earning respect and recognition of my preferred suppliers.

Create a list of suppliers that you want to work with.

- Choose your suppliers wisely based on your niche or the needs of your targeted market.
- Make sure the supplier is reputable and well-established.
- If you belong to a consortium, check the group's list of preferred suppliers.
- Do your homework on suppliers. Learn about the companies and their products.
- Find out what their commission tiers are. (Note: These are many times negotiable. I have found that if a supplier thinks that there is potential for sales and growth they may be willing to start you at a higher level. It's always worth asking.)

Request a meeting with your local DSM (District Sales Manager)

- If it is a supplier that I want to build a good future relationship with, I will often invite the DSM to meet me for coffee or lunch, at his or her convenience. This shows a sincere request on my part, and I am willing to compensate them for their time.

- First and foremost, come to the meeting prepared with a good business plan that explains how you would like to see the relationship grow with the targeted supplier. The business plan does not need to be elaborate. At minimum, have bullet points listing the basic goals for your business relationship.
- Show how your current or targeted customer database matches their products.
- Come to the meeting prepared to sell yourself and your agency to the supplier by bringing a portfolio or folder that you can hand to them that includes the business plan, a brochure on you and your agency, testimonials from both clients and other suppliers, and list any associations or consortium affiliations which you belong to.

Here is a sample of a starter paragraph from one of the proposals that I have made to suppliers and DSMs:

"Ticket To Travel's targeted community for marketing is made up of the ideal client who we feel will want to know about your product. This is a community of 1500 homes where the average home value is XXXXX. This affluent neighborhood is made up of families, couples and individuals who are active in golf, tennis, and travel quite frequently. I have selected your company as one that I would like to establish a business relationship because I feel that your product will match well with this audience.

"Suppliers now recognize the selling power of the professional home-based travel agent."

The surrounding communities will also be in my marketing plan, including XXXXX, an upscale retirement community of over 1000 homes. I have chosen these marketing demographics based on statistics that show that XXXXX is the fastest growing affluent area in XXXXX County."

All that most suppliers want to see is that you are making an earnest effort in building a mutually rewarding association. Once you establish a relationship with a supplier then other marketing opportunities will open up, such as, co-op marketing funds, product training and additional marketing alliances. Remember, as in any good relationship, respect needs to be earned and not expected.

Anita Pagliasso working with Hawaii Suppliers

Chapter 9 | TAX TOOLS

Running a legitimate home based travel business can reap many wonderful tax deductions. Unfortunately too many home-based agents end up paying the taxes every year because they are unaware of several small business deductions that are available.

Here is a list of some of the things you can deduct from your income taxes while running a home based business.

Host Agency Fees – If you join a host agency or purchase into a franchise, the expenses such as startup costs, monthly hosting fees, or franchise fees may be claimed as a deduction.

Business Supplies – Be sure to save all receipts for any supplies you purchase for your business use. Computer paper, business cards, stationary, or any items you purchase and use for your business. Do not overlook the small things like pens, paper clips and such. You might be amazed how all these little expenses add up at the end of the year.

Postage and shipping expenses – Any time you mail confirmations, invoices or other documents to clients, keep the receipts. This will also include any direct mail marketing pieces.

Advertising – Most advertising can be claimed on your taxes. Keep all receipts for any newspaper ads you may run. If you join a networking group, this is considered advertising and can be deducted as such.

Automobile expenses, gas receipts and mileage – The IRS allows take certain per mile deductions for each mile you drive when conducting business for your travel agency. Remember to log your miles every time you drive to see a client, go to a meeting, travel to attend a supplier seminar, drive to the airport to go on a FAM, go to the post office to mail business-related documents, or run any of dozens of other business-related errands.

Give-a-ways – Keep receipts and a list of any promotional items you may give away at shows or other venues. Any gift that you give clients may also be written off.

Phone bills and internet access – If you only have one telephone line, the IRS is usually not going to believe that you use this only for your home business since they consider the first phone line personal. A second phone line installed in your house will be 100% tax deductible. I would suggest that whether your second phone is a land line or a cell phone that you have a business greeting on the recorder. Internet service fees are deductible as a percentage depending on how much is for business use vs. personal use. (Are the kids surfing the web?)

Banking and Accounting – All bank fees and check printing for your business account.

Tax Preparation Expenses – You can deduct the cost of having your taxes prepared. Any accounting software that you purchase to help prepare your taxes for your business, such as QuickBooks, is also deductible.

Postage – All postage costs, shipping fees or shipping supplies may be claimed.

Computers and other equipment – If you purchase a new computer for business use, the cost of the computer may be claimed. You may also claim depreciation for 3 years after any equipment was purchased.

Insurance Costs – You may be eligible to deduct the cost of your health insurance premiums on your taxes. You are not allowed to deduct the insurance costs of your family members unless your family members are employees of your business. The cost of Errors and Omission insurance is also deductible.

Home Office Deduction – Your office at home and related expenses are allowed deductions according to IRS guidelines. To qualify, your home must be the primary place where your business is conducted. Additionally, the office space must be used exclusively for your business. Writing portions of your home off as a deduction as this is strictly a matter that should be discussed with a tax consultant. Although the IRS has become more lenient towards these types of deductions you will need to keep in mind that this is the one deduction that carries a cost with it, since when the home is sold, business owners may owe taxes on any depreciation costs they've deducted.

Entertaining – If you entertain clients while conducting business, even if it just over a meal or coffee, it is deductible. While you can only deduct 50% of the cost of meals and entertainment, it is well worth keeping records.

To use these tips you will need to follow these two rules:

1. *Prove that you are trying to make a profit*
2. *Keep good business records*

Advertising – Any paid promotions for your business. This also includes memberships for Chamber of Commerce and Networking organizations.

And of course, travel expenses! – The most important one of all: your travel. When you are traveling for your business, keep all receipts for plane fare, lodging, food, entertainment, etc. The number one question that I get asked about is FAM trips. If you are on a legitimate FAM trip, then yes, it is deductible. And exactly how does the IRS tell if it's a personal vacation or a legitimate familiarization trip. Be prepared to have on file site inspection forms, business cards of any representatives that you meet at the destination, FAM invitation, and a trip or two booked with clients to that particular destination? Any deduction you can't back up with a receipt, invoice or other substantial documentation, such as purpose of expense, will not be allowed in the case of an audit. Also, make sure to save your receipts for the correct amount of years as advised by the IRS.

AVOID BEING CLASSIFIED AS A HOBBYIST BY THE IRS

Try to avoid paying large amounts of taxes or owing any money by keeping track of expenses and business records.

In general, to avoid having your small business considered as a hobby and having your business losses and expenses disallowed, run the operation as a real business, under an accepted business structure, and work hard to make a profit.

To add to this list, another factor is the structure of the business. If it is set up as an LLC, partnership, or corporation, there is more likelihood that it will be viewed as a "real" business as opposed to a hobby.

Some activities are viewed more skeptically by the IRS than others. For example, a craft business or a travel business may often be viewed as a hobby, where a consulting business or professional firm might not be.

Here is a list of questions that IRS may use to define a legitimate business:

1. Does the time and effort put into the activity indicate an intention to make a profit?

2. Do you depend on income from the activity?

3. If there are losses, are they due to circumstances beyond the taxpayer's control or did they occur in the start-up phase of the business? The start-up phase can last several years, but there should be some progress toward profit during this time.

4. Have you changed methods of operation to improve profitability? In other words, have you cut costs, increased marketing activities, and found cheaper ways to produce and sell products?

5. Does the taxpayer or his/her advisers have the knowledge needed to carry on the activity as a successful business? That is, are you an expert in this area?

6. Do you have credentials, education, and experience in the field, rather than just time spent on the hobby?

7. Have you made a profit in similar activities in the past?

8. Does the activity make a profit in some years?

9. Can the taxpayer expect to make a profit in the future from the appreciation of assets used in the activity?

I realize that each of us may be running our home-based businesses a bit different, and I am by no means a tax advisor, so please be sure to mention any of these ideas to your accountant or CPA to see if your business can qualify for these deductions, which may be the key that can help put a little extra cash back into your pocket.

Chapter 10 | TECHNOLOGY TOOLS

IT'S ALL GEEK TO ME!

One of the most challenging aspects of running a home-based business is keeping up with the constant change in technology. It's easy to get overwhelmed with the pressure to manage your business, master new computer skills, become internet savvy, and learn all the new technical jargon. Things change so rapidly that it is hard not to feel that the time-consuming process of keeping current is more of a burden than an asset to your business.

Remember when…

"A Computer was something on TV from a science fiction show of note. A Window was something you hated to clean. And Ram was the father of a goat. Meg was the name of my best friend and Gig was a job for the nights. Now they all mean different things…and that really Mega Bytes! An Application was for employment. A Program was a TV show. A Cursor used profanity. A Keyboard was a piano. A Memory was something that you lost with age. A CD was a bank account.

And if you had a 3-inch floppy, you hoped that nobody found out. Compress was something that you did to the garbage…not something that you did to a file. And if you Unzipped anything in public, you'd be in jail for a while. A Mouse pad was where a mouse lived, and a Backup happened in your commode. Paste you did with glue. A Web was a spider's home, and a Virus was the flu and Twitter was something a bird did!

I guess I'll stick to the pad and paper and the Memory in my head. I hear nobody's been killed in a computer crash, but when it happens they wish they were dead."

--author unknown

This incredible machine has made it possible for me to run my home-based travel business in the most sophisticated of ways. The relationship I have with this piece of equipment, however, is more of a love/hate nature. I know that I am completely hooked on the Internet and realize that it would be impossible to run any home-based business without it. Yet I am the type of person who buys a car and could care less what's under the hood. I just want to put gas in it and go! I don't care how it works, as long as it works. It's the same for computers. When everything is working properly, it's the most amazing tool in the world. But when things go wrong, your workday and productivity are stopped.

I can sometimes be stubborn and think that I can somehow fiddle around and fix the mysterious maladies when they happen. I would spend hour after frustrating hour trying to understand what happened until I finally called the toll-free number for Microsoft Technical Support. It costs $35.00 per case incident, but they will stay on the phone with you as long as it takes to resolve the issue. One of my phone calls lasted more than 3 hours! Now, whenever I have a Microsoft problem, I don't hesitate to pick up the phone and call them.

I have also found a local computer repair store that promises a 24-hour turnaround on repairs. After I established a relationship with this store and got to know the technicians, it was easier to call up for advice on small problems.

When it comes to home office equipment, however, you can always count on something needing attention. Just as the computer issues get resolved, it will be more than likely that the paper in the printer will jam!

CANNING THE SPAM

On a daily basis, I can get anywhere between 200 to 300 pieces of junk mail. It clogs up my computer and my time. Even with the spam filter on Yahoo! as well as another on my virus protection product, I still have a huge amount of junk that manages to get through to my regular mailboxes. I have found a software program called "SonicWALL Mail" (www.sonicwall.com) that is the most effective at catching the majority of it. After a few automatic training sessions on what type of emails to "Junk" or "Unjunk" the program identifies the sender, analyzes the content, and applies a review to every similar email. Of the three spam filters I have,

SonicWALL effectively catches the biggest majority of the junk. If after scanning the Junk Mail folders and I find legitimate mail all I do is hit "Unjunk" and it will remember to allow the sender's future emails. For a mere $29.00 per year, it has been a great investment.

SMILEYS AND EMOTICONS :-)

A smiley is a sequence of characters that either follow the punctuation or takes the place of punctuation at the end of a sentence. A smiley is meant to tell someone what you really mean when you make an offhand remark. They are also called emoticons, because they intend to convey emotion, which the computer cannot do! Did you know that there are more than 500 of these types of symbols? These range from angry, embarrassed, surprised to YIKES!

ACRONYMS & TEXT MESSAGING SHORTHAND

These abbreviations are becoming commonly seen wherever people go online – including emails, instant messaging, PDAs, websites, newsgroup postings, and blogs. Just like the smileys, there are hundreds of these, such as LOL. When I started getting lots of reply email messages with LOL, I first thought people were telling me "Lots of Luck!", and I was starting to feel a bit insulted. It took me months to figure out that LOL means "Laughing Out Loud."

Hmm… Now I need to go back and reread those messages. Not sure which was more insulting – Lots of Luck or Laughing out Loud?

Out of the hundreds of these acronyms that I found on Google, my favorite was AAAAA – American Association Against Acronym Abuse.

TTFN – Ta-Ta for now!

GOOGLE, GADGETS AND GEEKS

I admit that over the years I have met a lot of extremely tech-savvy home-based agents. I am always envious of those who seem to quickly grasp the latest technology. With products changing as such a rapid pace, it's hard to keep up with the newest software, computers and gadgets. As hard as I try to stay abreast of technology, I seem to conquer a new program or piece of equipment just about the time that it is becoming obsolete.

> *"I seem to conquer a new program or piece of equipment just about the time it's becoming obsolete."*

A good example is when I recently purchased a new lightweight laptop for traveling, only to find out that two weeks later that someone came out with one that is even smaller and lighter. How are you ever going to keep up and know when it is the best time to make a purchase?

Equipment – Just like my cars, which I drive until the wheels fall off, at times it takes something breaking down before I upgrade equipment. When my old printer spilled its last drop on ink on my carpet and jammed its last bunch of paper, I finally broke down and

purchased an all-in-one fax/printer/copier/scanner. *Why did I wait so long?*

I can now scan articles to save for future reference, print high quality pictures and eliminate extra pieces of equipment from my office, thus allowing me more space. These types of combination units are not all that expensive anymore. (I think the manufacturers make most of their money selling the ink).

Most office equipment, including computers, has become fairly reasonable. Over the years, I have realized to run a professional business good tools and equipment are a must. Consider this equipment as a cost of doing business.

Staying connected – I recently dropped my cell phone in water (don't ask!) and was without a phone for a few days. It made me think about a recent incident at the airport reminiscent of a time before cell phones. I couldn't help but notice a man waiting in line, frantically pacing and crying. I went to him to see if I could help. He was a foreign visitor who could not speak English but in Spanish he told me he could not find his family and his flight was about to leave. I felt so bad for him but my first thought was "Where are your cell phones?" It was then that I realized how convenient and easy cell phones have made our lives, especially in instances such as in this.

After drowning my phone I did purchase a fairly "techie" phone. However, getting me up and running took many phone calls to my new "friends" at tech support, and now I really love all of the features of this phone. It's also a pocket PC, which allows me to send and receive all of my Microsoft Outlook email through the phone. The downside is that it doesn't filter junk mail, but I have found that I can easily scan through the incoming messages and read only the pertinent ones. It gives me a head's-up to what I may need to address when I return to my office, as well as the ability to respond immediately to anything urgent. Because it also synchronizes with my Microsoft Outlook calendar, I no longer need to carry around an appointment book. This small device has it all, including the ability to download and run Power Point presentations, create MS Word docs, and more.

Yahoo Groups, (groups.yahoo.com) has been an invaluable communication tool for many of the networking groups and associations to which I belong. Once you join, all messages can be sent to the group for all to review or respond. There are also areas for uploading files, photos, taking polls, for the group's usage and reference.

Google has allowed us to essentially throw away phone books and encyclopedias that used to collect dust on our book shelves. Now a world of information is at our finger tips. Type in a few descriptive words in the search bar and viola, there it is. How many times have you read that a hotel is on the beach to find out it's across the street from the beach? Or maybe you need to find a hotel close to an airport or cruise port. With using Google Earth (http://earth.google.com) you can see satellite images of actual buildings and surroundings. Using the zoom function, you can see the beach, palm trees, pool, parking lot and even the closest Burger King.

Gadgets – OK, I admit that am not that good on keeping up with the latest electronic gadgets. I'm one of those who still can't program the… Oops…I was going to say VCR, but I think that is pretty much outdated now. But I did find a pair of slippers that have a connection you can plug into your computer's USB port to keep your feet warm under your desk. Now here's a gadget I can actually use!

Part II

POWERFUL MARKETING

Chapter 11 | STEPS TO MARKETING SUCCESS

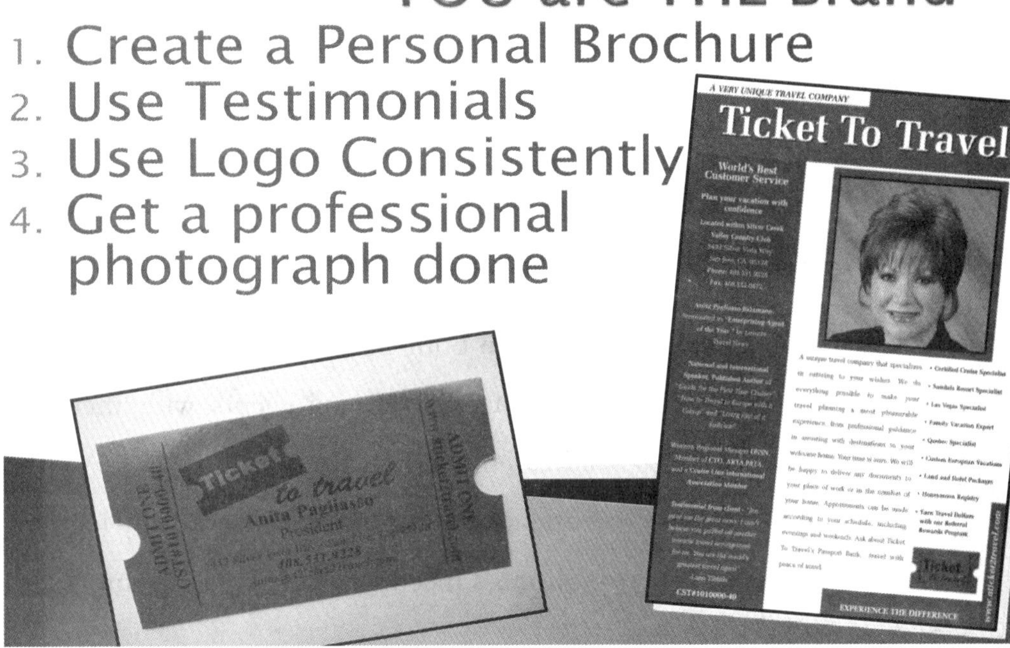

CREATE A BROCHURE FOR YOUR BUSINESS

Before you hand out that supplier's brochure, make sure you hand out a brochure of your own. Use a software program such as Microsoft Publisher and create a brochure about yourself and your business. If you don't have the Microsoft Publisher software you can go to http://office.microsoft.com/en-gb/templates/default.aspx for the Microsoft Office Template Gallery which offers over 3000 templates for calendars, resumes, greeting cards, business plans and lots more. When putting together your own business brochure, make sure to include the following:

- Point out the features that make you stand out from all others in your field.
- List all of your credentials.

- Include a picture of yourself.
- List all of the associations that you belong to.
- Include testimonials.
- Brand yourself with a unique logo that is consistent in all marketing pieces.

BE A WALKING/MOVING BILLBOARD

When I go to my local Curves to workout, my t-shirt and baseball cap both have my agency logo. When I carry my mail to the post office, I put it in a canvas tote that has an enlarged version on my logo on both sides. I also order these same canvas totes to give to my clients with their documents thus enlisting them as billboards as well. I carry a briefcase and portfolio that has my logo on it to all business meetings. Here are a few more ideas:

- Wear an interesting piece of jewelry or other items you purchased while traveling as a conversation piece.
- Magnetic car signs that include your company information.
- Personalized license plates or license plate frames.
- Order some customized stickers and put them on every item given to your client.
- Take airline tickets out of the paper advertisement they come in and put them in customized ticket jackets with your agency's information and logo.

FIND A POWER PARTNER

A "Power Partner" is someone who has a different business but often the same customers. You can have a mutual agreement to refer business to each other and often times work jointly on particular events or presentations, such as sharing the cost of a booth at a bridal fair with a wedding planner or photographer. You may also agree to share databases and cross promote.

- Mortgage broker and Realtor
- Dive Schools and dive shops for dive travel specialists
- Wedding Planners / Photographer / Beauty Saloon
- Web services and networking company
- Limousine company and event planner
- Mary Kay and Weekenders

GET OUT OF THE OFFICE!!

Working from you home you can be assured no one is going to come knocking at your door to find you. You will need to get out among the buyers. Find venues to let people know you are in the business of selling travel and what your specialty is. Join organizations such as:

- PTA
- Rotary Clubs, Lions Clubs
- Bunko, Women and Men's Clubs, Bridge Clubs
- Church / School Groups and Clubs

NETWORKING AND BUSINESS LEADS EXCHANGE

The idea is simple – members gather for regular meetings to enjoy a meal while learning about each other's businesses and professions, as well as exchanging leads and contact information. Check the business calendar section of your local newspaper or publications for times and locations for these types of meetings in your area.

- Local Chamber of Commerce
- Business Leads Groups within the Chamber of Commerce membership
- Business Leads Unlimited
- Le Tip International – www.letip.com
- Leads Clubs – www.leadsclub.org
- Business to business social mixers.

BUILDING A TRAVEL BUSINESS THROUGH NETWORKING GROUPS

Several years ago I decided that even though my business had grown substantially thanks to word-of-mouth, it was time to take it to the next level. Realizing that advertising can be extremely costly, I needed to make sure that I got the best return for my investment. Of course, there were newspapers and various other forms of media, but that meant competing against dozens of other travel companies. Another option that surfaced was to join a local "Networking Club".

The following outlines what I found in my research and why it turned out to be one my best business decisions ever.

What is a Networking Group?

These groups provide effective business networking opportunities that link together individuals who, through trust and relationship-building, become walking, talking advertisements for one another.

The weekly, hour-long meetings are run by and for the members with the sole purpose to exchange referrals for new business. The meetings include open networking; short presentations by everyone; a longer, more detailed presentation by one or two members; and time devoted solely to passing business referrals.

Memberships are typically limited to 30 per chapter. This gives everyone an opportunity to get to know the name behind the business cards, thus allowing for more comfort and trust in giving referrals. Membership is also limited to only one person per business category in each chapter. This means that there can be only one realtor, one chiropractor, one plumber, one travel agent, and so on. Creating a non-conflicting atmosphere and also eliminates any competition for referrals for travel business.

> *Clubs bring together professionals across all fields for referrals and shared opportunities*

The organizations operate by charging reasonable annual fees, averaging between $150.00 and $300.00 per year. Additional costs may include meals at the meeting location or minimal fines levied for various reasons, including not bringing a lead or referral for a fellow member. When I did my analysis, however, I found that these annual fees were often less than the cost of running just one newspaper advertisement.

What are the Networking Rules?

Since you will be required to give leads and referrals to other members, you will want to know that you are associated with reputable businesses. For the members' protection, references are required, and there are ethical sets of business standards to which all members must adhere. This will assure you that that the members are successful business people who are not only good at what they do but also ethical in the way they conduct their business.

- Regular attendance at weekly meetings is required. Because a limit on absences is enforced, only dedicated and motivated business people are attracted.
- Members must meet with others on a one-on-one basis to learn as much as possible about them and their business.
- Dedication and willingness to assist others in their business growth is equal to your desire for support from them.
- Members must demonstrate a sincere commitment to developing at least one qualified lead per meeting for any fellow member.

What are the Networking Benefits?

- There will be weekly opportunities for exclusive advertising promotion of your business.
- Other Members work to provide you with qualified business leads. Most will be carrying around your business cards to hand out to those who could use your services.
- These groups are considered an advertising service, thus membership may be tax-deductible.
- You effectively gain a personal "sales force" of up to 30 others committed to helping you succeed by not only giving you their own personal business but also referring their friends and associates to you.
- There are also opportunities to increase your ability to communicate effectively and become a better public speaker.

To find a group in your area, check the business calendar in your local paper. You can also use a search engine and enter "networking groups." Many of the major groups have nationwide chapters. Before selecting a group, however, visit as many as possible in your area. Many will allow you to visit twice before joining. Because of the attendance requirements, take into consideration the location and time of the meeting. While visiting, listen to the tone and attitude of the group, and take note of the camaraderie.

Here are a few to take a look at that are likely to be in your community:

- **Business Leads Groups within your local Chamber of Commerce**
- **Business Leads Unlimited**
- **Le Tip International**
- **BNI – Business Networking Intl.**
- **Elite Leads Inc.**
- **Business to Business Social Mixers**
- **E-Women Networking**

Does all of this take a commitment on your part? Yes, but if you want your business to grow substantially, as mine did, the rewards of attending one networking meeting a week far outweigh the time or money invested. Some of my largest groups, which have included mayors, and local officials and personalities, have come from my networking efforts. I can't imagine how I would have had these opportunities were it not for the exposure given to me through the networking clubs and organizations that I belong to.

Anita Pagliasso is second from the right at a Chamber of Commerce Ribbon Cutting for Red Robin. The gentleman in the center rear is the San Jose Fire Chief.

Anita Pagliasso volunteering at a Veteran's Day Parade with city officials.

AMC Theatre Ribbon Cutting with the President of the Chamber of Commerce

---

WORKING THE ROOM!

How to build your travel business at local networking events

On a couple of occasions lately I found myself in places where I felt I could to do some serious networking. Networking can serve as a valuable strategy for getting new business and is how I have grown my business. But most of us are not born to mingle, including myself. It took lots of practice and preparation to develop the skills it takes to be effective.

As difficult or awkward as it may feel at first, the ability to meet and make a positive, professional impression on people will become ever more important as your business grows and develops. Here are some tips to get you started.

> *You can't work a room when you're sitting down.*

Get an attitude check – Many of us are shy and often reluctant to approach strangers in new social situations, so understandably it's not always easy to muster the energy to try and connect with people at networking events. That's why it's key to get mentally geared up before you even show up. Since your attitude often guides your behavior, you must overcome any negative self-talk that could hinder you from reaching out to others. But if you change your attitude from negative to positive, you can take the lead in changing this.

Remember – People enjoy talking about themselves, and love talking about travel. Ask them questions to get them started. People feel flattered when you show a sincere interest in them. You have more to offer others than you might think – just believe it.

Redefine what it means to interact with strangers – When you join a new organization or networking club, you share certain interests and objectives with the members of that group. Try to view a networking event as an occasion to find what you have in common with other people. Commonalities help "strangers" connect more easily.

Take the initiative in approaching others, introducing yourself, and sharing a piece of information that could reveal the common thread you share with them. During conversations, listen carefully to discover shared interests or goals. Use your shared background or interests as the basis for sustaining conversations.

Practice your introduction to make it clear and interesting – To avoid being tongue-tied when you try to start a conversation with someone you don't know, prepare a self-introduction that is clear, interesting and well delivered. An introduction shouldn't take longer than 5 to 10 seconds. And while practicing your introduction might at first seem silly and artificial, it will eventually help you develop one that sounds natural, confident and smooth.

Here are a few examples – "Hi, my name is Gale Infeld. I'm glad to have this chance to meet you. I specialize in family adventure travel." "Hello, my name is Martha Powell. I put together group fund-raising cruises that benefit nonprofits." These short introductions give a clear message about the type of business that these agents are looking for.

Know that rejection is not the end of the world – It happens. Some individuals may not respond to your introduction in the way you would like. If that takes place, don't take it personally and just move on.

As long as you maintain an outgoing and friendly attitude, you can plan for continued networking success by trying these techniques. Identify the goals you want to achieve at the networking event before you go. Keep a healthy sense of humor. Treat everyone as you would want to be treated. Arrive early. If you're one of the first in the room, you can adopt the mindset of someone who is there to meet and greet, as opposed to walking into a room of 200 people who are already talking to one another. Wear something that can make for a conversation starter, such as an unusual brooch or lapel pin that you picked up during your travels or is travel related.

Focus on being approachable and make it easy for people to talk to you. Attend every event with the intention to have fun. Imagine that the next person is an old friend you haven't seen in years. Smile and shake his hand as though he were that person.

And last but not least, don't forget how important it is for you to physically move around and about when you're at a networking event. Remember, you can't work a room when you're sitting down. So get in there and show them what you've got!

BECOME A SPEAKER

If you have difficulty with making presentations or standing in front of an audience, join a local Toastmasters Club. (www.toastmasters.org). I have found just about any group that meets on a weekly or monthly basis, would be interest in having someone speak about travel, whether is about destinations, tips for the first time cruiser, travel consumer rights, or updates on safety and security issues. Believe it or not, I once did a presentation for an association for CPAs. I timed it for right before the height of tax season, knowing that when April 16th hit, they would all be ready to go somewhere to relax. Here is a small list of potential speaking opportunities.

- Rotary Clubs
- Business Associations
- Senior Centers
- Country Clubs
- Conferences and seminars

30 SECOND MARKETING

Going up? Take your elevator speech to the top!

They are often called elevator speeches and are intended to prepare you for very brief, chance encounters in an elevator. But elevator speeches are not just for elevators! An elevator speech is a short, 15-30 second, roughly 150-word sound bite that succinctly and memorably introduces you. It spotlights your uniqueness as well as focuses on the benefits you provide. This is something that should be delivered effortlessly. It's also an excellent way to market yourself and your services.

Who else, other than you, can describe with passion, precision and persuasiveness what you do? A great elevator speech makes a lasting first impression, showcases what you do and allows you to position yourself for meeting new potential clients.

If you want to network successfully, you will need an elevator speech!

When I first started joining networking groups, I laughed to myself when they said that part of the benefit of joining as a member would be that each week I would get 30 seconds to make a presentation. 30 seconds? Big whoopee! What in the world could anyone convey in a mere 30 seconds?

After attending a few of these meetings, however, I quickly learned that it is vital to be able to make your point in concise terms and quickly. People judge a person on first impressions. Therefore, it only takes a few words for someone to form an impression.

WHY ONLY 30 SECONDS?

Often during an introduction there is only time for a few words so they better be the right ones. People nowadays are busier than ever and because of this they tend to have shorter attention spans.

Think about radio and television advertisements, which are typically from 30 to 60 seconds. Advertisers pay top money for these spots so it is essential to get across the right message. It must be short, succinct and get exactly to your marketing point.

KNOW YOUR STUFF

At my first networking meeting it never dawned on me to prepare anything…after all it is only 30 seconds and certainly thought I knew my stuff. Boy was I wrong! Going around the table, one by one, members were delivering these powerful little 30 second presentations. As it was getting closer to my time, nerves took over when I realized that I should have prepared something. When I stood up, I stuttered out something like "Hi, I'm Anita and I sell cruises and vacations." PERIOD! My mind totally blanked out and I couldn't think of another thing to say. I sat down horrified and embarrassed.

How to create a great "elevator speech" that makes a lasting impression.

I was never going to let this happen again, so I went home and worked on it. My little 30-second speech took hours to create. I wrote and rewrote it until I had the message I felt I wanted to get across.

Your own elevator speech must roll off your tongue with ease. Practice in front of the mirror and with friends. Record it on your answering machine, and listen to it. I rehearsed mine until I knew it by heart. I taped it to my steering wheel in the car and on my way to the meeting I said it over and over. At first I felt silly so when I would come to a stop sign I would put my cell phone up to my ear so people didn't think I was talking to myself ☺.

HOW TO PREPARE AN ELEVATOR SPEECH

First, and most important, think in terms of the benefits your clients or customers derive from your services. Think about what you want to portray. Are you a destination specialist? What destination? Are you a "travel agent" or are you a "cruise and vacation planner, specialist or consultant"? It's a subtle difference but unless you want to be constantly asked during an introduction how much it costs to fly from Cleveland to Chicago, I suggest you *don't say you are a travel agent.* The better option would be to put the thought of a vacation or cruise into their mindset as to the type of business that you are looking for.

"Who else, other than you, can describe with passion, precision and persuasiveness what you do best?"

First, write down the special extra services that you provide. Then, think in terms of the benefits that your clients could derive from these services. Once you've got that written, create an opening sentence that will grab the listener's attention. The best openers leave the listener wanting more information.

Do you sound confident? Sincere? Is it engaging? If not, keep tweaking until you are clear on what you want to say.

- The structure of an elevator speech is similar to a prepared speech. There is an opening, body and ending but the organization is very tight.
- There is no time to ramble or tell stories. You need to be brief, clear and enthusiastic.
- Make sure to explain why someone would benefit from your services.
- Avoid using travel industry jargon.
- Try to differentiate yourself from the competition.
- Summarize what you do in one simple and clear sentence. (Your hook)

HERE'S HOW I IMPROVED MY SPEECH:

"Hi, I'm Anita Pagliasso and I have been a cruise and vacation specialist since 1992. I love planning trips of a lifetime for all of my clients. In fact, last year I saved most of my client's money over the internet pricing while also providing them special VIP service, throughout the planning process to their welcome home. I also gave them with the assurance that should anything go wrong during their travel I would be available at all times to assist them. If you enjoy traveling I would love to give you my business card."

Now, you've got their attention!

Hint: Have your business cards handy at all times so that you don't have to dig or fumble looking for them. I also wear my "networking suits" to business events that have pockets where I can keep a stash of cards ready for a "quick draw" at any time.

Remember, these quick effective 30-second spiels are not only great for networking events, they can also be used at PTA meetings, business functions, fundraisers, in line at the movies, getting your morning latte, and almost anywhere you are likely to meet new people – even in an elevator!

IT'S IN THE CARDS

Small yet so powerful! One of the most overlooked advertising tools a home-based agent can have is a small, inexpensive rectangle piece of paper – the business card. It is important to remember that when you hand someone your business card, you are making your first impression. That's why you want your card to be attention-getting, pleasing, informative, and memorable -- so people will look at it, comment on it, pass it around, and keep it handy for future reference.

NO MORE PALM TREES!

During my various marketing seminars, I collect business cards and give away a prize for the most creative design. I am always astonished at how many of the cards look so much alike and it has often been difficult to find cards that stand out. I would say that 80% or more of the cards I have collected include a palm tree or a cruise ship in the design. This is certainly a safe and common choice but does nothing to make you stand out.

DESIGN, IMAGE AND BRANDING

My travel agency's name is Ticket to Travel so I designed my business cards to look like a bright gloss-red ticket with notches cut out on both ends. I have arranged all the pertinent information on the card in the style of a performance ticket. Because of their uniqueness and bright color, my business card actually becomes an easy topic for starting a conversation and brands my business by using my ticket logo.

We are in the business of selling dreams, adventure, relaxation, romance and fun. Your business card design should match your business model. Is your specialty or niche leisure or corporate? Cruise or adventure? Family or senior travel? All-inclusive or FIT vacations? Make sure your card conjures up these types of immediate images.

MAKE YOUR CARD UNIQUE

Your business card is an overlooked advertising and marketing tool.

Here are a few ideas:

- Dive specialist – Have cards cut in the shape of dive goggles.
- Honeymoon specialist – Cards in the shape of a heart, but use a Caribbean or tropical theme and color palette.
- Cruise specialist – How about cards die cut in the shape of a ship?
- If you still want to use palm trees, why not make it the shape of your card?
- If multi-color processing is too expensive, have standard type cards printed on gloss coated colored paper stock rather than white stock.

USE 100% OF THE SPACE

If you paid for a full page ad in a paper you wouldn't leave it half blank. Consider using 100% of the entire card, including the back. If you need more space, fold over cards can be used effectively as a mini-brochure to point out what makes you different from every other travel agent, including a brief description of credentials, such as CTC or ACC.

Many people who receive cards like to jot memory-triggers on the backs of cards. Why not cleverly print your own memory message on the back, such as:

Met at:__________________

Date:__________________

Note to self: Call for planning our next vacation. Offers outstanding customer service, pricing and personal expertise. Most grateful for referrals.

CONTACT INFORMATION

Remember, the main goal of a business card is to make an impression and give an easy means to contact you for future business. Include a business number, email and website address. You may want to include a cell phone or home number. Giving out this type of personal information builds trust when trying to establish a new relationship. Since most everyone now communicates through email, I no longer find it necessary to include a fax number.

CONVEY YOUR MESSAGE

Don't forget to convey what kind of business you are looking for. If you put the title "Travel Agent" under your name and you only sell trips to Hawaii, you will waste this advertising opportunity and your time having to tell someone you don't book airfare to Cleveland. Decide which information is absolutely essential and persuasive. Just as important, too much information can dilute your message.

DON'T CUT COSTS

My business cards are more costly than the traditional stock cards, however, I can't recall a time that I handed it to someone and didn't receive a comment about how nice or unique they are, thereby accomplishing my goal to get the client to look at the card and the information offered. This is not an area where you want to cut costs by printing your own on perforated template business card stock purchased at office supply stores. The quality rarely looks as good because the material is flimsy and the perforations aren't finished, leaving ragged edges. Cheap looking cards do not portray professionalism or seriousness about your business. Make sure that you

> *"Make sure that you invest in the best business card design that you can afford."*

invest in the best business card design that you can afford as this will be your introduction to a new client and the low cost per card will be money well spent.

STICK OUT LIKE A SORE THUMB!

How to attract attention to yourself and your travel services

This should be your new marketing mantra: Be very noticeably different, particularly obtrusive, conspicuous, blatant, prominent, and attract undue attention or notice. To sum it up, stick out like a sore thumb!

In other words, become "American Idol's" William Hung of the travel industry. "American Idol" had thousands of great singing contestants that year, but Hung was definitely one heck of a sore thumb. Everyone was scouring the Internet to find more video clips of him, be it spoofs or interviews, and his quirky audition ultimately did earn him much popularity. I would say that his fame was fueled by just how remarkable he was and by people's habit of sharing the latest interesting news with their friends. You would want such extensive exposure for your business, wouldn't you?

Just like the "American Idol" auditions, today the marketplace is crowded with smart and talented travel businesses. We should all agree that without constant exposure, your target market wouldn't even notice that you're out there. So how is it possible to get yourself spotted? The answer is that you need to become remarkable yourself.

Agents can easily get too involved in the day-to-day operations of their business and not spend any time brainstorming new marketing ideas or promotional events. Some may worry that marketing is too expensive, while others may find it too time-consuming. Without announcing who you are and what you sell, how will anyone know? Have you ever wondered how you can become remarkable? Here are a few ideas:

Create a tagline for your business – You can do this on letterhead, fax cover sheets, emails and invoices. Mine say "Your Cruise and Vacation Concierge" in a slanted banner across the top. And my email signature includes every award that my agency has garnered, such as "Best of the City" or "Reader's Choice Award."

Use client testimonials about your services – If you haven't achieved any awards as of yet, include a brief testimonial from a client. One of the first testimonials I received was from a client who said I was "the best travel agent in the world!" That testimonial still resides on my website.

If a client gives you a referral, spotlight that customer as your "Customer of the Month." Be sure to advertise this in numerous places, such as your newsletter, emails and website. Send that customer a thank-you letter and a certificate for a discount on a future vacation or cruise.

Host a special VIP event – You can do this for your best customers, and ask them to bring guests. It can be part of a new cruise ship preview, a destination theme or just a happy hour. Other sample events that can help increase sales include talks on such topics as "Learn insider traveling tips from a travel pro" or "How to pack for a week in a carry-on." There are numerous events you can host, and so be creative and have fun. Keys to planning successful special events include setting goals, promoting and marketing the event, and offering booking incentive specials.

Draw attention through "sign spinning" – You've all seen them. Businesses spin and throw their arrow-shaped signs like batons, strum them like guitars, paddle them like canoes, ride them like horses—anything to grab the attention of passersby—with messages such as "large pizza today $5" or "furniture sale—70 percent off." This form of advertising, called "sign spinning," emphasizes the here and now, pulling local traffic into a grand opening, a big sale or a special event.

Make yourself stand out at tradeshows – Next time you're participating in a bridal fair or business expo, do something unique to stand out. I remember a particular dive conference that I was asked to speak at a few years ago. I realized that I knew nothing about dive travel but I wanted the participants to come see my presentation. Keeping with the oceanic theme, I handed out small plastic fish to everyone. Inside the mouth of the fish was a rolled-up note that said "Fishing for great marketing ideas? Get hooked up at Anita Pagliasso's presentation!" When people saw I was giving something away, a crowd gathered just to see what all of the buzz was about.

If you really want to distinguish yourself from everyone else, be remarkable in your very own way. William Hung sang, "She bangs! She bangs!" And so will you if you make your marketing stick out like a sore thumb!

Chapter 12 | DIALING FOR DOLLARS

Many of us have a database full of people that have never booked a trip with us. We have gathered contact information from other clients, bridal fares, networking meetings and just about any place that we could grab a business card. When I sold electronics many years ago it was a common practice for sales people to use this information to do "cold calling" to drum up new business.

But "Cold Calling" implies something less than warm and pleasant. The word "cold" is used because the person receiving the call is not expecting a call or has not specifically asked to be contacted by a sales person. I prefer to think of it more as "Dialing for Dollars".

These calls should be used is a filtering process. Just like panning for gold or digging for diamonds, you have to turn over a lot of dirt before you find the gems. I know this will sound odd, but your objective in making these calls is to "disqualify" as many people as possible, as quickly as possible. By eliminating these people it will save you time and money wasted on sending brochures and marketing pieces to people who will probably never buy a trip from you.

You will only have about 30-45 seconds to deliver a specific and compelling reason for the person on the other end to "want" to continue the conversation. It's best to skip the small talk and get right to the point.

A few essentials:

- Tell them your name and company.

- Ask permission for 45 seconds and tell them they can end the conversation after that if they want to.
- Get right to the point.
- Help them identify their previous travel problems by offering a short synopsis of what you have done for existing clients.
- Ask open ended questions.
- Never try to convince a prospect, instead let them convince you it is worth your time and effort to meet with them.
- Honor your agreement and let them off the hook if they do not want to engage.

Here's an example of a call:

"Hello! My name is xxxx and you gave me your contact information at (example: xxx Travel Show). May I take a minute or so of your time to tell you about my travel agency and what I do special for all of my clients? I work with travelers who are looking to be treated to great customer service and who may be frustrated with the lack of personal attention from the large online travel companies. With my expertise and guidance, I sort through all of the options to make sure that you get exactly what you are looking for in the way of a vacation or cruise. I'd also like to clear the common misconception that it costs more to use a travel agent. The truth is that more often than not I will save you money. I work with all of the major travel companies and cruise lines, and my reputation is excellent. If you don't mind sharing I would be very interested in hearing about where you have traveled in the past? What are your favorite and least favorite things about traveling? If you think we can work together in the future, may I continue to stay in contact with you?"

Make cold calling a regular task to identify potential customers

In less than 45 seconds you will know if you have someone on the line who you can help or not. If they do not have any problems that you can fix, then it's over (for now). Remember, they may not have plans to travel today, but they may have it in their future. And if there is a possible fit, then you can set an appointment to explore the future possibilities of working together.

The best thing about "cold calling" is that you do not have to do it forever. Once you have a client-base and they are more than satisfied with your products and services, they will, with your nurturing, become promoters of your business and you will have more referrals and less need for "cold calls".

We live in a world of email overload so I would also suggest that you periodically pick up the phone and give your existing clients a personal call. But remember to follow my number one rule…just call to say "hello"… DO NOT ask for business or referrals this time. Maybe ask how their last trip was or for any suggestions on how you can make the experience even better next time.

You can break down your database and devote one or two hours a week to accomplishing this. If you make "dialing for dollars" a scheduled event in your calendar and you do it with consistency you will be amazed how much new business you will do.

Chapter 13 | CREATING SUCCESS STRATEGIES

Sometimes it is tough to tell what works when you're selling. You may be saying to yourself "I know that half of my marketing efforts may be working, I just don't know which half". Let's face it, marketing requires time and money. That's why we want to use options that develop the most new business.

Listening to the experts can sometimes cause even more confusion. A public relations firm will undoubtedly suggest more media coverage and advertising, a graphic designer may tell you that you need a new logo and better brand identity, database management companies will indicate that you must have targeted direct marketing and, of course, a web designer will urge you build a better website or to boost your search engine ranking.

> *Don't be afraid to try new and even risky strategies to build your business*

The truth is that successful marketing requires all of these options and possibly even more. Indeed, I've found that many times home-based agents can get overwhelmed thinking that they have to do all of this at the same time, which couldn't be further from the truth. Implementing one marketing idea at a time it will allow you to better track its success.

Several years ago I received a call from a local senior citizen center looking for sponsorship for their weekly bingo games. At first I said "no" because the advertising price was higher than I had allocated in my budget. This was my first lesson in negotiating advertising costs because the more I said "no" the lower the cost went. That was the good news. The bad news was that I did not get one call from this promotion!

It was obvious to me why my ad didn't generate any interest after seeing it in print. Instead of being in a publication, the ad was printed on Bingo pads in small grey font, which most seniors would never be able to read. Plus, the only thing that the ad included was my logo, the fact that I was a cruise and vacation specialist and my contact information – but there was no "call to action".

CREATE A CALL TO ACTION

The next time when one of my agents was interested in advertising at an "Over 55 Living Community" we made sure that the ad was actually in a newsletter or another type of publication and that we could have a quarter-page with large bold fonts and relevant images showcasing the travel product we were selling. We decided to promote a cruise that was sailing round trip to Alaska from San Francisco, so we headlined the ad in large bold font that said **"DRIVE TO YOUR NEXT CRUISE!!!"** We kept the wording minimal so we could utilize larger fonts and we highlighted our contact information. We sold out our group space, and so the ad had measurable success.

I also have participated in my consortium's direct marketing program with much success. Not only have the mailing pieces brought my agency new business, but they also have led to more brand recognition and consumer awareness for the market that I want to reach. By taking advantage of these mailings on a consistent basis, I was able to see the payoff in many ways. Because these mailings went out to a targeted geographical area close to my neighborhood, it branded me as the neighborhood "go to" travel company.

> *"Implementing one marketing option at a time will allow you to better track its success."*

As is true as in many of the other rules in the travel business, the 80-20 rule should apply towards marketing as well. Establish an annual marketing budget and allocate 80% of those funds to the tried-and-true methods that you have used in the past, but try investing 20% in new ideas and tactics. Ultimately, your goal should be to try to stay ahead of the trends and not try them only after they have become successful for your competition.

Don't forget that working closely with preferred suppliers will give you an annual marketing co-op budget will allow you to expand into many of the new areas that you might not afford to do so on your own.

It's a normal reaction to stick with what is safe and what has worked in the past. However, the travel industry is ever changing, and the marketing options are always evolving with those changes. If you only stick to what has worked in the past and fail to try new marketing strategies, you will slip you into mediocrity and the competition will eat you up. Don't be afraid to build some element of risk into your marketing plans. The businesses that are most successful are those who are willing to take some calculated risks and take a leap of faith.

GOT BOGO? WHAT'S GOING BEHIND THOSE "BUY ONE, GET ONE FREE" OFFERS

By now I'm sure everyone has seen the catchy commercials for Payless Shoe stores. BOGO is "buy one, get one half off" at Payless. Before the Payless campaign, BOGO was an acronym that was universally known in the marketing industry but rarely presented to customers in this form. Originally, "buy one, get one free" was a sudden end-of-season or clearance method used by shops with a large quantity of stock that they were looking to sell quickly.

BUY ONE
GET ONE
FREE

"Buy one, get one free" or "buy one, get one" is a common form of sales promotion today in the travel industry. Two-for-one travel promotions have become quite popular recently, particularly due to the economy. Some cruise lines have marketed sailings such as the "2 for 1 Escape the Economy Sale."

The good news about these types of sales is that they offer great marketing opportunities that can generate inquiries and new sales. Such promotions are meant to get consumers' attention. For example, Payless' ad campaign has been successful because it draws people in to get the deals, especially new customers. But what do you do after the BOGO offer draws them in? Whether it's buying a pair of shoes or going on a first cruise, the marketing campaign isn't fully successful unless customers become repeat clients.

I recently had an experience where I was delighted to score my own "BOGO" deal. Each year my friend and I celebrate a mutual birthday. Rather than exchanging gifts, we treat ourselves to an evening out at a nice restaurant. This year it was my turn to pick the restaurant. I happened to choose Morton's Steak House simply because I received an email promotion that offered two three-course steak dinners for the price of one.

We were greeted by our hostess, who said, "Welcome to Morton's Anita and Patricia! We are honored that you chose to dine with us on your birthdays. I hope you didn't have any problem finding parking. I tried to call you to warn of possible traffic snarls since there was a parade downtown earlier in the day."

We were then escorted to our table by a maître d' and immediately introduced to our server. From the moment we walked in I felt we were treated like royalty, but I thought, "What's going to happen when they find out we're "coupon" ladies?" A bit embarrassed, and not wanting to surprise the waiter, I thought I better let him know early on that we would be using the BOGO. "That's great!" he said. "When I return with your drinks I will tell you about your choices."

Along with our drinks, he brought us personalized printed menus that included the message "Happy Birthday Anita and Patricia!" As our drinks appeared, so did another staff member with a camera. "May we capture the evening for you?" As a perfect ending for our birthday dinner, we were presented with a complimentary dessert and the photos signed by all the wait staff.

This was my first time dining at Morton's, and from the time we arrived till the time we departed the service, employees, food, and overall dining experience well exceeded our expectations. To top it off, the next day I received a follow-up call from the manager thanking us for our visit.

Morton's made us feel like very special customers. My friend was so impressed that she asked if I brought all my friends and clients there because of all the attention we were shown. Morton's is fortunate to have such fun, energetic and passionate employees who really do care about their customers. What I especially liked about the service was that it wasn't a "forced" friendly, but it felt truly genuine.

This isn't meant to be a commercial about Morton's but more an example of how we can all learn by taking a look at a successful company's mission and core values. In Morton's case, its mission is to "always exceed our guests' expectations." Its core values are based on the idea that only the best will do for every guest. "We value each other. We will offer only the finest products. We strive to consistently improve every day, in everything we do. We expect to be profitable."

Based on these values, I have come up with a new acronym for BOGO that we can all use. In this case, BOGO stands for:

Best Products for Valued Clients
Outstanding Service
Genuine Caring and Hospitality
Operate Profitably.

THE BUTCHER, THE BAKER, THE CRUISE AND VACATION MAKER

Win more business by learning a few lessons from your neighborhood realtor and other local businesses

On a regular basis I am asked "*Can you really make a living running a travel business from home?*" The answer is definitely yes, but, only if you are willing to really get serious about marketing yourself. If you want to take lessons from some of the best marketers out there, take a look at your neighborhood realtor and other local businesses. On the average, a person moves only once every 7 years. But knowing these statistics does not deter the realtor from marketing to you from the first day you move into your new home. You will get post cards, recipes of the month, calendars, market updates, community events, lists of recommended local businesses and regular newsletters. And I am certain that you have all received the post cards with pictures of homes marked "sold" in bold letters across the advertisement.

Why would they waste the paper, printing and postage to show you a property that was no longer available? It's their way of sending you a testimonial of one of their successful transactions. And all of this correspondence will surely include a picture of the realtor. Why? All this is an effort to position their image so that their name and familiar face will be the first to pop up. Maybe not now, or 2 years from now, but in 7 years when you become that statistic and may be ready to sell or buy a new home. They are investing their efforts and advertising money in hopes of getting your future business.

Translate this into the travel business. How often does the average person take a vacation? The answer is roughly once a year. Does that mean that you only should contact them only once a year? Not in today's competitive market. You need to be first and foremost in their thoughts when it comes time to plan their vacation.

One way to do that is to become marketing partners with your neighborhood realtor. Just by asking, I was given an excel database from my neighborhood realtor who was also targeting the same area. In return I gave her discount travel coupons to put in her "Welcome Baskets" for new homeowners. To get the attention of the new neighbors, I put the coupons in envelopes that I had made from maps and on the outside of the envelope I created a large sticker that read, "Welcome to beautiful Silver Creek…NOW GO AWAY!!!

Ask other neighborhood realtors to get on their lists of recommended businesses. I have successfully partnered with other neighborhood businesses that regularly send out local advertising. This gives both businesses an opportunity to co-op with producing a joint marketing piece to cut down on costs. Wherever your neighbors shop is where you should concentrate on such cross promotions. Contact the editor of your local or neighborhood newspaper and offer to write a travel column. Set your goal to become known as "The neighborhood cruise and vacation specialist."

Unless you live in a rural area, try focusing your marketing around a 10 mile radius. Believe it or not, I learned this business strategy from a window washer!!! I hired this company strictly because his advertisement was targeted specifically to my housing development. He detailed what he could do that they competition couldn't, and he quoted prices by the names of the specific models of the homes. When my daughter wanted to utilize his services, he politely refused saying that he only worked in my community and that was how he could provide great service and low pricing. You see, his travel time and expenses were minimized by only going to one area. He could also service more homes per day than his competition that were spending a large amount of their time getting from one appointment to the other. He was successful by focusing his business on what he knew best, namely my neighborhood of 1500 homes.

> *"You need to be first and foremost in your neighbor's thoughts when it comes time to plan their vacation."*

How successful would your business be if you could be the vacation and cruise provider for just 5% of everyone who took vacations within a 5 mile radius of where you live? According to the San Francisco Insider, there are 15,000 people per square mile in San Francisco, New York has 24, 000 and Los Angeles has 7,000. If, like me, you follow my realtor and window washer's advice, you also will find success right in your own backyard.

WIN-WIN MARKETING

One day I was listening to a radio broadcast that actually changed my whole outlook on building my business. The guest on the talk show happened to be the head of a job placement agency and the discussion was about the high numbers of people out of work after the dot com crash.

A caller looking for advice and compassion stated that she had been out of work for eight months with no luck whatsoever. The guest spoke up in a strong voice and said "You are NOT out of work. You have a full-time, eight-hour a day job. That job is 'looking for work.' You have to get up, get dressed and get out there by 9:00AM and don't stop until 5 or 6:000PM."

It struck me immediately that this philosophy should also apply to my business. I couldn't complain about the lack of business since it was my job to find work for myself. Boy – did this burn in my brain! Ever since that radio show, I have made it my number one priority to go out and constantly find ways to cultivate new business.

It's not enough just to take care of current clients or rely on word of mouth. To grow, or even just maintain a business there has to be an ongoing sales and marketing campaign using new and fresh ideas…especially in the fiercely competitive environment of the travel industry.

How cross-marketing with businesses in your area can lead to winning results

Most recently, I have been approaching other businesses to co-market efforts with me. I started with spas and have worked my way through many businesses such as clothing stores, scrapbooking stores, art galleries and even a dental office! I wasn't just any dentist, however. I approached a specific dental office because of its own unique approach to marketing.

"Tranquility Dental Spa" offers an experience quite different from the traditional dentist office. When was the last time you looked forward to seeing a dentist? Well, picture this:

You walk into a waiting room that is filled with sounds of soothing music and calming spa aromas. Next, the receptionist offers you herbal tea and a list to select your choice of a first-run movie to view during your dental treatment. Next your hands are dipped into a warm moisturizing wax treatment and then slipped into soft mitts. As you sit down into the plush soft leather reclining chair, you are handed the controls to what you find out is a $5000.00 massage chair.

"I create a proposal for each meeting outlining the benefits of co-marketing with my travel agency."

I took one look and immediately knew that I wanted to approach the dentist to do some co-marketing efforts. I was sure that the clients who went to this dental office were potential customers who would also appreciate a five-star vacation experience along with my VIP customer service.

Of course, I never go into a business appointment unprepared or empty handed. I create a proposal for each meeting outlining the benefits of co-marketing with my travel agency and also include my personal brochure and testimonials. To my surprise, these businesses were extremely receptive. In fact, when I arrived at my appointment at a large Spa, I started to pull out my proposal and portfolio and before I had it out of my briefcase, the manager of the Spa opened the proposal that he had put together for me.

As a result of these cross-marketing efforts, I have been able to put on events that were held at business locations where they even provided all of the food and refreshments. How does it work? We both invite our respective clientele to an event. My co-marketing business partners offer interesting demonstrations related to their business along with a discount on future services or goods. I make presentations on a variety of interesting travel related topics and give a gift certificate to each new prospective client to use toward their first vacation or cruise booked through my agency. Thus, creating new exposure for both businesses and a "Win-Win" marketing strategy!

Marketing Partners

ANITA'S PROPOSAL FOR CO-MARKETING OPPORTUNITIES

- **Mutual business growth development by co-marketing to the same demographic market**
- **Joint promotions such as, Spa nights, Spa and Wellness Getaways.**
- **Cross marketing each other's databases**

CO-MARKETING MARKETING PROPOSAL

What We Envision	Results
Event invitations through co-marketing to both databases	Exposure to a new audience of potential new clients in the same demographic market
Display material	Offer a predominate place to display promotional material, brochures and future trips
Informative Presentations	Offer education in beauty, wellness, health and various aspects of travel
Exclusive offers for attendees	Events will allow opportunities to cross-promote products – may offer discounts and promotional products.
Develop Mutual Marketing Opportunities	Examples could be at expos, networking events, booths, conferences, etc.
Cross-Marketing	Increased business and profit from strategic marketing alliance.

Chapter 14 | POWERFUL MARKETING IDEAS

MARKETING FUEL TO KEEP YOUR MOTOR RUNNING

Don't run out of gas when you think of marketing ideas. Maybe you are finding that what has worked in the past may no longer be enough to keep the influx of new business coming in. Challenge yourself to try new approaches and ideas. Here are a few of my marketing ideas that may give your home-based travel agency the tune up it needs.

Specialize in golf or sports packages – Go to golf course clubhouses and country clubs and offer to make a presentation as an expert on various golf resorts as vacation destinations. Most country clubs have speaker series events for their members.

Offer a honeymoon registry – One thing we can always count on in the travel industry is that people will continue to get married, have big weddings and go on wonderful honeymoons. Approach bridal and tuxedo shops, florists and photography studios and offer to host a "Bridal Registry" information night. Explain how friends and relatives can contribute to the honeymoon of their dreams through your registry program. Use a slogan such as "What sounds better, a toaster or Tahiti?"

Honeymoon Groups and Destination Weddings – I have successfully suggested to wedding couples "Why not take your friends and family with you on your honeymoon cruise?" After they look at me like I am crazy and stop laughing, I explain "You will still have your own private honeymoon stateroom or suite but instead of dining with strangers on the cruise, why not continue the wedding fun with friends and family?"

Get in front of an audience – Go to your local libraries, community colleges, churches and offer to speak about your specialty, current travel trends or travel tips and advice.

Create a video for YouTube – If you have a specialized group or trip you want to promote, create a video to showcase it. It doesn't have to be done in a studio, but you will need to get someone who can at least hold the camera steady. Tri-pods are inexpensive for this use. I recently did one of these in front of my Ticket To Travel banner at a conference. We had to re-do it a few times, but it turned out pretty good and it was fun.

Services for Men – Advertise a travel presentation "For Men Only." Cater to the men who have the means but lack the imagination to come up with that "special" package for the person in their life. Your service can include not only travel but a package that includes all the frills such as airport limousines, champagne, flowers, restaurant reservations, tours, plays, etc.

Men's Travel – You can expand your services to offer sports packages, Harley-Davidson riding vacations, Dude Ranches, hiking, boating and fishing trips. Go to a local Harley-Davidson shop and ask to put on a presentation and also to display your brochures. For racing fans offer packages to race tracks for hands on, high speed, behind the wheel action. I have clients who are die-hard NASCAR race fans and will travel all over the country to follow the race circuit; however, they also stay in 5-star hotels.

Women's Travel – Start your own club for women travelers. Put together trips to destinations that specialize in gardening, cooking, wine tasting, exercise, art and museums. One of my most successful women's trips was a tour that I customized that went to the same cities in Italy as were in the book and movie "Under the Tuscan Sun".

Join your local Chamber of Commerce – You will have many opportunities to network with prospective clients and speak to audiences about your business.

Family travel – Go to large corporations that have child care facilities for their employees. Ask if you can make a presentation on "How to enjoy quality time on a family vacation" or

"How to effectively of combine business and family vacations - mixing business with pleasure."

Start a Countdown – Create excitement and urgency when a new ship is coming out. As soon as you know the date that the cruise line will start taking reservations, start sending out literature and follow up with countdown mailings and emails.

Host a Cruise Night – Contact your local cruise line reps for assistance with special discounts if they book during the evening. I have hosted very successful Cruise Nights right in my home.

Sport and fitness travel – Go to a local day spa or gym and ask if you can host come in and speak about Spa Vacations. Also ask if you can put your brochures on display.

Family reunions – Cruising is great for reunions. You can arrange for special cocktail parties for the group. A photographer can be arranged to take pictures. Everyone, of every age, has some activity that should appeal to him or her.

Take advantage of supplier's free email marketing – They are professionally done and meet all of the "opt out rules" for spamming. All of the call-to-action has your contact information. Many times I send these out and it is just the reminder a client needs to contact me to set up their next cruise or vacation. Just by keeping in front of your database will give you the edge over the competition.

Direct mail campaigns, thank you cards, handwritten notes – Use the US post office. Many of my agents have shown up to 30% increase in their business when regularly sending out direct mail pieces.

Ask for referrals – Let everyone know that you would appreciate any referrals. I know a realtor who includes "Thank you for your referrals" on all of her correspondence and business cards.

Regular maintenance is vital to keeping your car out of the shop, and it's just as important for your business. Make sure your business batteries are kept at full charge by trying a few of these ideas. Your business will stay revved up and continue to move forward towards the finish line.

What Would You Do With $100?
Try these great marketing ideas that won't put a huge dent in your budget

A lot of agents think that effective marketing has to be painfully expensive. So let's say you only had $100 to market your business using one campaign. What would you do? How creative and innovative could you get on such a small budget?

By setting a budget, and getting creative with your marketing, you can add a significant boost to your business

- Use $100 to get quality business cards designed and printed. Always carry them with you and give them out freely. Ask permission to leave them in places your target customers may visit. Print the products you sell or services offered on the back.
- Go to a local restaurant or shop and offer to sponsor a drawing for a $100 gift certificate or a product. Use the entry forms to collect customers' mailing addresses.
- Take $100 to develop and print brochures that feature your expertise and the services you offer.
- Find a non-competing business to co-market with and hold monthly or semi-annual seminars about a travel product or service you offer. Give the seminar an enticing title like "Learn Insider Traveling Tips from a Professional Travel Consultant." Use $100 to provide food and beverages.

- Purchase $100 worth of T-shirts with your logo and website to give to your best customers. They become walking, talking billboards.
- Use the $100 to take a few of your major clients out to lunch to thank them for the constant stream of business and loyalty.
- Donate a $100 travel gift certificate to a charity event or auction.
- Buy $100 worth of note cards and postage. Send hand-written thank-you notes to important customers every chance you get.
- Purchase brightly colored envelopes and unique stationary for sending direct-mail pieces or documents.
- Budget $100 to use for a Facebook ad or pay-per-click advertising. You can control exactly how much to you want to spend and how often. In most cases you can set your own budget and how often you want the ad to run. There's no minimum spending requirement – the amount you pay is up to you. For instance, you could set a daily budget of $5 to run for 20 days, or $20 to run for five days. Both options equal $100.
- Create a loyalty program to reward existing customers. Use the $100.00 to offer a credit toward future travel. As an example, you could create a loyalty card for clients that gets stamped for each cruise booked, and when they book their fifth cruise they get $100.00 off of their next cruise. Use your imagination based on your market.
- You can market online for free, but you may not have the time to do all that you'd like. For $100 you could hire a virtual assistant to update blogs, articles, press releases and all your social networking sites.
- Spend $100 at a local "dollar store." Store up on client gift items such as games, books and beach items to keep the kids and everyone entertained and happy while on vacation.
- Postcards are a wonderful marketing investment because they're so versatile. You can use them to announce specials, celebrate customers' birthdays or for many

other creative events. The recipient doesn't have to decide whether or not to read your mailing; as soon as they see it, they've read it.

- Buy personalized "bon voyage" labels or stickers that include all of your contact information. Put them on all gifts, document holders, etc.
- Market your professional image and buy a new suit with the $100 to wear to business meetings.
- A table or show space usually costs around $100 to $200. By sharing space with a non-competing business, you can participate in the costlier ones.
- YouTube costs nothing to use, and webcams or Flip videos are now within the $100 price range. Friends and family may be able to help provide great dialogue and music. YouTube marketing provides the audience. All you have to do is get creative. People are motivated by videos that create an emotional response and personal connection. Personality and enthusiasm is sometimes hard to convey on fliers but can come through on a video.
- People love to belong to special groups, such as an insider's or VIP club. Use $100 to source a company for custom cards that identify their club status. Offer "insider" monthly travel specials.

By setting a budget, and getting creative with your marketing, you can add a significant boost to your business without putting out the big bucks.

Low or No Cost Marketing

- Auto responder on your email with a message regarding a current promotion.
- Add an advertisement on your phone message. "Ask me about our special cruise to Alaska".
- Email newsletters on a monthly basis. Keep yourself in front of your customers.
- An e-cast regarding a special promotion or news item of interest to your clients.

INNOVATIVE AND FUN MARKETING IDEAS

Products and ideas to use for target mailings and promotions

I once used actual plastic baby bottles to mail invitations out for a baby shower. I filled the baby bottle with pastel colored confetti and rolled the invitation inside. I pre-typed the adhesive stick on mailing labels that went on the outside of the bottle. The cost was minimal to mail each of these, but what a response I got. Friends talked about these invitations for the longest time. I figured if this got such a great response, why couldn't I come up with some creative ways to promote my travel business in the same way.

What follows are samples of some promotional ideas that will get the responses you will want at a minimal cost. Many of these items can be put inside of a regular letter-size envelope and they need no extra postage.

As long as the item is not breakable, almost anything can be sent with just postage. How about sending a personalized coconut with a thank you note painted on it to that client who just booked an ocean view suite in Hawaii? Sound crazy? Maybe, but do you think they will ever forget this? Do you think that they will tell their friends what they got in the mail from their travel agent? And that's the whole point.

Ways to put some fun in your targeted mailings and promotions!

If you have an idea for a mailing and are not sure, take the item to the post office and ask what it would cost to mail it as is, without wrapping it or putting it in a box. That is what I did with the baby bottles and many of the other promotions. Sometimes I will even mail a promotion to myself first to see exactly how it makes it through the mail.

I never send out anything in plain white or manila colored envelope. In my opinion, this is way too boring for a travel promotion and very likely to be tossed the junk mail pile. If you need to send your promotion in a package, choose something unusual. There are bright-colored mailing envelopes now that are lined with bubble wrap. You can order bright colored boxes. Draw pictures or put travel related stamps on the outside. Try anything to make it stand out from the rest of the mail.

I have purchased most of the following products for my marketing mailings I have purchased from a discount catalog, where you usually can by merchandise by the dozens at almost wholesale prices. But you can also find many items like these in dollar stores, discount stores, and flea markets.

Here are some of the fun and effective marketing mailings that have been successful for me:

- **Inexpensive duck puppets:** I included a note that said "Do you need to get out of town before you quack up? Call us quick!"

- **Globe stress balls:** "Relax, go ahead and use this stress ball, or better yet, let us take care of sending you away to be pampered at a luxurious spa."

- **Wild animal key chains:** "We have the key to your wildest dreams."
- **Wild animal book marks:** Don't just read about it...Let us help you live your own adventure trough travel."
- **Magic wand with tinsel:** "Just like magic...we will make all of your travel wishes come true."
- **Funny paper glasses with sleepy eyes:** "Have you looked in the mirror lately? Maybe you need a vacation? Call us before it's too late."
- **Plastic hand clappers:** "Go ahead and give yourself a hand! You've worked hard and deserve a break. Relax now and let us work for you. Where in the world would you like to go?"
- **Paper airplanes with dollars printed on them:** "Don't let your money fly out the window. We make sure you get the best value for your travel dollar."

Just use your imagination. I happened to find some flower seed packets of "Forget-Me-Nots" in a dollar store. The total cost was only 10 cents each. I printed some small labels with my agency information and logo to put on the packets. I also added a note which said "We look forward to growing our business with you." This could also be used to send to a client who you haven't heard from in a while. You could write "I haven't heard from you in a while. Please remember that I am always available to assist you with your next vacation."

I hope these ideas will get your own creative juices going. Remember that you are in the business of selling fun so don't be afraid to let your imagination and sense of humor soar.

Chapter 15 | PRESENTATIONS, EXHIBITING AND SPEAKING

PREPARING TO PRESENT

Several years ago, I was invited to make a presentation to agents at a large conference in Las Vegas. While going through the show program, I saw how many participants were expected. The more I focused on the numbers, the more nervous I became. **I worked myself into a frenzy. My heart pounded, my hands trembled, my knees knocked, and for the first time in my life, I began to hyperventilate!** I'm not sure how, but I pulled myself together and made the presentation, although a bit shaky in the beginning.

Since that first frightening experience, I have spoken to thousands of agents, Rotary Clubs, radio stations, business and networking associations, chamber of commerce, and travel schools. But I wasn't able to do this before making a deep analysis of what I needed to do to improve my speaking skills. I also found out that there were many techniques to lessen my **"stage fright."**

BE PREPARED

The biggest error I made during that first presentation was not to have prepared or rehearsed properly. Rehearse? It didn't even occur to me. I was sure that I knew my material, as the ideas and success stories I wanted to share with my audience were from my actual experiences. But when I went to open my mouth, I couldn't find the right words to get started. And even worse, when I referred to my notes, the words didn't sound the right when spoken out loud. Getting more nervous by the minute, I was certain that I was going to pass out. I was starting to see the headlines: **"Speaker dies on platform...*literally*."**

For the next presentation, I vowed to be better prepared and to rehearse properly. At first, after hearing myself speak out loud, it felt very awkward. But then I said the lines over and over until they became familiar. I continually adjusted to find words and phrases that I felt comfortable saying. I learned to take out anything that didn't feel right coming out of my mouth. In other words, I practiced until the presentation flowed like a conversation.

Speaking to large groups need not be a frightening experience.

It is also helpful to ease nerves to find out in advance how a room will be set up. Get comfortable with the setting, check out the layout, and make sure everything is ready for any audiovisual needs. When you are nervous to begin with, the last thing you want to happen is to have technical problems.

JOIN TOASTMASTERS

After seeking out recommendations, I joined a local chapter of Toastmasters (www.toastmasters.org). At my first weekly meeting, I met about 15 people who were there solely to improve their speaking and leadership abilities. It turned out to be a very supportive and fun environment where I could practice the new skills and techniques we learned. Each person in our group was from a different career field, which made the meetings all the more interesting.

Conquer the Fear Factor of Public Speaking

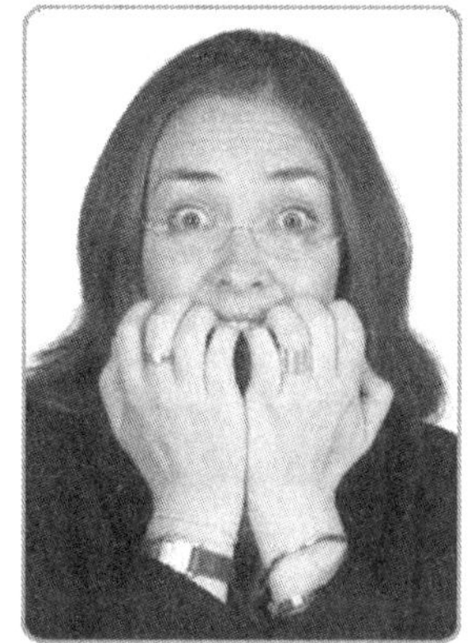

Get in front of one client or a group

•Making a sales pitch to a potential client or group.

•Speeches like these are important to your career, and you must perform them well.

For 84 years Toastmasters has helped people conquer their speaking fears

www.toastmasters.org

MEETING AND GREETING STRANGERS

For many, the most uncomfortable situation is walking into a room full of strangers. Now you have to give a speech to these strangers! Talk about a double whammy stomach churner. Try not to think of them as strangers. Somehow, you have something in common with them. Maybe it's a community, your membership in an organization, or a networking group. You also have to remember that they are there because they really want to hear what you have to say.

I have found that arriving early allows me time to get to know my audience. I once served as the "greeter" as attendees arrived, and people were surprised and pleased to be welcomed by their speaker. You could also walk into the audience as they are being seated and introduce yourself to as many people as possible. "Nice to meet you" "Thank you for coming." Shake their hand with a firm handshake, make eye contact and smile. Look at their nametags, make a comment, observation or ask a question. Above all, be genuine and sincere!

The people with whom you have just chatted will pay attention because you're no longer just a presenter; you have created a personal connection. When I make eye contact with one of my new acquaintances, I notice that they are usually the ones paying the most attention and also participate the most during the interaction sessions.

MAXIMUM EXPOSURE

If you have been to any of my presentations, you know how much I encourage everyone to take as many opportunities as possible to get in front of an audience. I have found that most of my largest clients have come from speaking opportunities. Making presentations to groups, no matter how small or large, is an excellent way to promote yourself and your business. This allows you to interweave your credentials, insights, and value while giving the audience knowledge, thus allowing you to build trust and become the **"expert"** in the room.

IT'S SHOW TIME!

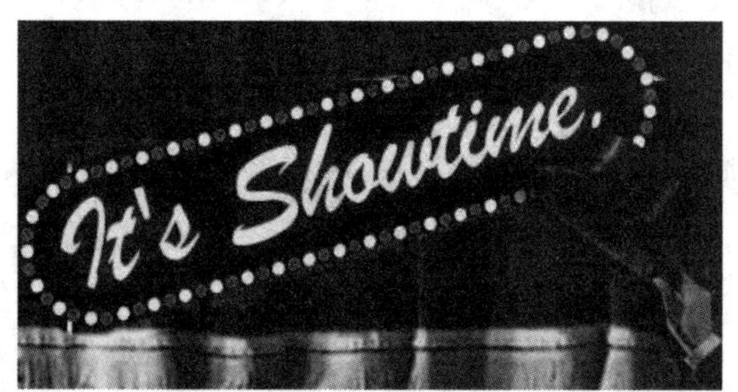

As an agent at home, I'm a big believer in taking your business out on the road. This means finding all types of different opportunities to showcase your travel agency at expos, bridal fairs, flea markets and just about anywhere potential travelers will congregate. Here are some ways to get your business noticed in the marketplace.

Planning

No matter what type of an event you plan to participate in, planning well in advance will assure the most success.

Supplier partners

This is where it becomes all important that you have a set of preferred partnerships with specific suppliers. Having a good business relationship will be an asset when you are looking for cooperative funds to help pay for the cost of exhibiting and providing collateral material. If I am promoting a particular supplier or cruise line, I will often ask my sales representative to come work the show with me.

Supplies and Set Up

You must take stock of what you will be showcasing well in advance of the event. One thing I try not to have on the table is brochures…yes, brochures. I keep those in the back to use when I am engaged in a conversation and have already profiled the potential client. Included on the table, it will be my own personal brochure that highlights my specialties and certifications, along with lots of testimonials and a business portfolio. What I do request from my preferred suppliers is a customized, one-page flier detailing an ***exclusive offer*** available only through my agency – such as a shipboard credit, upgrades or other amenities – if they book within a certain timeframe. The attendees will be drawn to a special offer if they think that it is something they won't be able to get elsewhere. Another benefit of having a customized flier is that all of call-to-action information has my agency's contact information. If you do pass out brochures, make sure to use labels and not ink stamps. I once attended a bridal fair to check out the competition. There was an agency that had nothing but stacks and stacks of brochures. Brides-to-be were clamoring around picking up everything and anything. The agent working the booth sat there and kept handing out brochures, never engaging anyone in a conversation. From outside appearances and looking at the crowds that gathered, it

How to promote your business by taking it on the road!

looked like the show was a success for this agency. When I picked up several of the brochures and looked at the back, it was obvious that either they were in a hurry to get these done or they had paid the neighborhood kid to do it. In more than a dozen brochures that I picked up there was not one that was legible. Even if someone wanted to contact that agency, there was no way to do it.

Decorate with flair

It works really well for me to take a six-foot table at home and lay it out in advance to plan the design and content of my booth. Remember, you're not selling life insurance or vacuum cleaners, so make your booth fun and inviting. If it is a bridal fair, you will need material from your preferred supplier that has a romantic flare. I once poured sand over the corner of our table and bought sandals that left a "Just Married" imprint in the sand. We ordered pencils from a low price catalog that had my website imprinted on the side and wedding bells on the top. If it's a cruise night, I like to create an atmosphere of going on a cruise by throwing lots of streamers and balloons around the booth. For a beach resort feel, I throw Hawaii print pareos on the table top and put a grass skirt around the table.

> *"No matter what type of an event you plan to participate in, planning well in advance will assure the most success."*

Capturing the Data

If you want to capture a database of potential clients from the show, the best way is to offer a drawing for a prize. This can be anything from a gift basket you put together to a small piece of luggage to dinner for 2 at a local restaurant. Invest in an acrylic ballot box found at one of the major office supply stores. It will have a stand up slot on the top of the box where you can customize a sign for the show and what you will be drawing for. Then create your entry forms to include name, address, phone number, email address and where they are interested in going on their next vacation.

Staffing

If you work alone, ask a friend or spouse to come help you out for the event. There will be times that you will need to leave the booth, if only for a bite to eat.

Follow up

If you do not have a plan to follow up with the database you have acquired, you might as well stay home and save your money. Make it a priority to enter the information into a database program as soon as possible. Send an email or letter within a week of the show to let them know it was a pleasure to meet them. As a thank you for stopping by your booth include a discount coupon to use towards their next cruise or vacation package. Don't get discouraged if you don't get immediate results. Remember, many of the attendees may not have been ready to book their travel immediately. Be persistent with regular communication providing travel tips, special offers and additional information on your services. Your investment will eventually pay off. When the time comes for them to book their travel, it will be likely that your name will then come to mind. I have had people hold onto my business card from an event and contact me two years later to book their travel.

BRIDAL FAIRS 101

According to Condé Nast Bridal Group, every weekend some 45,000 Americans tie the knot and approximately 85% of these couples took a honeymoon at an average cost of $5,200.00. The question is, "Are you getting your share of this lucrative market"? One viable way to reach these prospective honeymooners is to participate in bridal fairs and expos. I have compiled some tips that have helped me prepare for these successful events.

Collateral material

Order brochures early and make sure that they are delivered no later than a week prior to the show. My preferred brochures are one-page flyers. They are easier to carry home and less likely to be thrown out. In most cases, my preferred suppliers have been more than willing to create custom flyers geared towards honeymoons and romantic travel for these show and may even pay for the cost of printing.

Booth Neighbors

Your guide to success when exhibiting at honeymoon and wedding shows

Make sure you know who your neighboring booths are going to be. Try not to be next to jewelry sales, timeshares, or any other companies that may distract brides and grooms from coming to your booth. Also stay away from booths with big spinning wheels or those who are giving away lots of free stuff so that people are standing in line in front of your booth to get just the freebees and blocking potential honeymooners from getting your information. Don't be afraid to immediately lodge a complaint with the show promoter should something like this happen.

Know your competition

Ask the show promoter for a complete list of all participants. If the list shows other travel agencies, go to their website and find out what they specialize in and make sure to focus on other products. For example, if you know that a large competing agency is going to promote nothing but Sandals, then focus on other products like cruises, Europe, Hawaii and other popular honeymoon destinations.

Booth Set-Up

Arrive early and allow yourself plenty of time to set-up. I bring props, such as several silk palm trees, colorful open suitcases to hold flyers and a bag of sand and flip flops that say "Just Married" on the bottom. I cover the table with tropical and colorful pareos. We keep only a few key brochures on the table and the rest are put under the table to keep the table from looking cluttered. I leave room for my portfolio and personal brochures. I leave an open space for brides to register or make an appointment for a free consultation.

"Make personal contact with each bride who stops at your booth."

Network with Other Vendors

Before the show opens, or while brides are viewing a fashion show, is a good time to walk around and introduce yourself to other vendors. Many of these same vendors may be great candidates for future co-marketing opportunities and some of the best referrals that I have received from these shows have been from other vendors. There is nothing like "word of mouth" recommendations to build trust.

Learn How to Break the Ice

The most important part of a bridal show is to make personal contact with each bride that stops at your booth. Handing out flyers is not enough. Be prepared to speak with as many brides as possible and make the most of the few minutes they may be willing to spend in your booth. The typical response to "May I help you?" is "No, I'm just looking." Don't set yourself up for a negative response. Instead your question should be, "Have you started planning your honeymoon yet?" or "What is your dream honeymoon?" Now you have broken the ice and can go on to talk about what you do special for honeymooners.

Prizes and Giveaways

Key chains, pens and other giveaways randomly stacked create the grab-and-run behavior with attendees. The best way to use giveaways is after a conversation present the item as a token of your appreciation. Create special entry forms for a large travel related prize or basket that include all of the needed contact information, as well as desired honeymoon destination, wedding date and estimated budget. This is an excellent way to gather information for your database.

Follow Up

Make sure to immediately send a "Thank you for visiting our booth" note which includes bullet points of your special services. It also reflects to the bride that you're reliable and efficient. Set regular intervals to send future correspondence as some of these brides are visiting shows a few years in advance of their actual wedding date. Bridal shows are an investment of time and money and not following up would be simply a waste of both.

Part III

People POWER

Chapter 16 | CUSTOMER SATISFACTION

ROMANCING YOUR CUSTOMERS

How you can meet the emotional needs of today's travelers

You can buy a date flowers, wear your best clothes and use your best grammar, but even Godiva chocolates won't be good enough without that certain chemistry. If you can't relate to your customers, then you may find them getting up, splashing the fine wine in your face and asking to speak with another agent.

Customer courtships can be fickle. Travelers have plenty of other agents and options waiting to romance them away from you – and some are more effective than others.

With a broad choice of places to buy travel, they can opt for convenience when that suits their needs, shop price on the Internet when that's most important or get special services when these amenities seem most attractive.

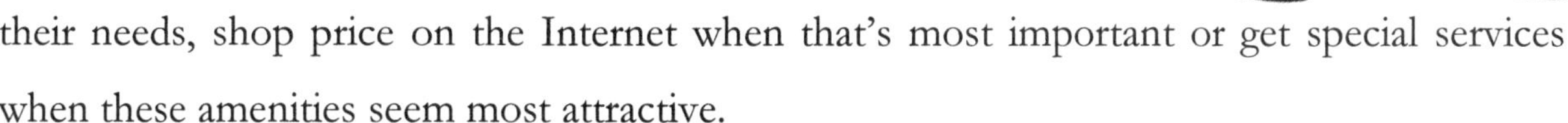

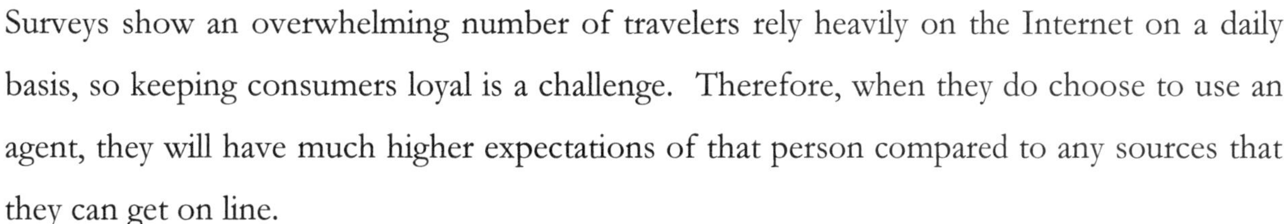

Surveys show an overwhelming number of travelers rely heavily on the Internet on a daily basis, so keeping consumers loyal is a challenge. Therefore, when they do choose to use an agent, they will have much higher expectations of that person compared to any sources that they can get on line.

Servicing a client means showing empathy if something goes wrong, and then offering a quick response. Empathy is the degree of caring and individual attention provided to clients.

You may not be able do anything about the fact that the airlines lost their luggage, but you can show them that you care. Responsiveness is the willingness to help clients and provide prompt service. This may mean something as simple as writing a complaint letter to the airlines on their behalf.

Agents who understand that they need to provide outstanding service but also satisfy the emotional needs of clients will continue to grow. Starbucks is a good example of a company that has tapped into this expectation. The coffee chain has created a warm, friendly environment that's safe and comfortable. No wonder it's so popular with first dates, which also makes it such a good choice as a place for home-based agents to meet first-time clients.

The process of buying and selling travel has undergone radical changes over the years and so must the delivery of service. Today's client is no longer looking for a purchase only, but also for an experience along the lines of those provided by Neiman Marcus or Nordstrom. Furthermore, travelers' preferences can change constantly and can vary by many factors, such as budget, "keeping up with the Joneses," radio and television ads, family dynamics, aging and abilities—just to name a few. That's why we should continue to monitor our clients' lifestyles.

A way of distinguishing ourselves from our competitors is by providing high-quality service, and also striving to create a friendly rapport, ongoing communication, trust and credibility with clients. Paying close attention to their changing needs means a better relationship. Once the client feels an emotional connection has been established, they develop trust.

Building trust in any relationship is paramount for loyalty. I can remember an incident I experienced with a couple of travel agents that I used before I got into the business. I quickly lost trust with the first agent because she took my credit card and never told me about the additional fees that she added to the reservation. I guess she thought that I wouldn't notice, but I did.

I bought my first cruise from the second agent and was very impressed by the manner in which she made me feel that meeting my needs was important to her. I gave her my payment and considered it a done deal. About a week or so later she called and told me that she saved me an additional 5%. She could have easily kept that as a bonus commission, but I believe she knew that the key to building successful relationships is about building trust. She certainly earned my trust.

An example of trust would be agreeing to go on a blind date set up by a person you know well, based on your confidence in that person's judgment. Using a client's trust to your benefit is another excellent reason to always ask for testimonials and referrals.

To back up your clients' trust, you must demonstrate your reliability and provide what was promised. In other words, clients are delighted when we do what we say we will do, when we communicate regularly and when we provide them with something new or of value. In any relationship who doesn't love surprises, gifts and spontaneity? So try romancing your best customers by sending flowers or a small gift just to say thank you and let them know that you care about their business.

APPRECIATION OF THE UNEXPECTED

When was the last time you sent an unexpected card at an unexpected time to a client? Do you think it would make a difference? Do you remember your client's birthdays and other special occasions? Do you think that matters to them? How about a simple thank you or expression of appreciation?

This doesn't have to be a daunting task. Besides the full featured database management programs, there are a multitude of other options for tracking and maintaining this type of client information. Microsoft Outlook has a multi-function calendar that allows you to put in dates that have weekly, monthly or annual recurrences. You can set the reminder to alert you within minutes or days in advance. There are also many online companies, such as www.birthdayalarm.com, that will not only remind you but also allow you to create and send out personalized electronic greetings.

Each year as my birthday approaches I try to take notice of what the companies that I do business with do on this occasion. This year I have received greeting cards from Southwest Airlines, my doctor, Chico's clothing store, Macy's, Sephora Cosmetics and others. I look at each of these greetings to try to learn marketing strategies that I can try to incorporate into my own business.

Southwest Airlines included a free drink coupon for my next flight, and I loved what Sephora Cosmetics did. When I stopped in to make a purchase the week before my birthday the sales clerk entered my transaction and then looked up at me and said "Happy Birthday, Anita. You get a special gift today in celebration." Not only did I get a nice gift, but five other people in line were also now wishing me Happy Birthday.

From the department stores, both Macy's and Chico's included a coupon as a birthday gift. Macy's offer was a $10.00 discount on any purchase over $30.00 and Chico's offered a $10.00 gift card with no limitations on any amount to spend. Both are enticing but I believe Chico's was more effective from a marketing standpoint. Chico's knows full well that the gift card will get me in the store but, based on my previous buying patterns at their store; it is more than likely that I will far exceed spending $30.00. This is a similar tactic to what I have done, which is to offer my best clients a birthday credit to be applied towards their next cruise or vacation. These amount of the credit can vary from $25.00 up, based on their past travel history. I actually had a client who booked a $10,000.00 family cruise and used the $25.00 credit coupon I had sent him.

It is obvious that these large companies are fully utilizing their database systems, which more than likely have automatic processing that sends out the greeting cards. Even so, there have been a few that stood out because there was something that made it special or more personalized. For example, I was somewhat touched by the card that I received from my Kaiser doctor merely because I realized that she took a moment out of her busy day to hand write a personal note. Her greeting card included the Kaiser logo but also included her picture and business card. And then she signed it "In good health." Is my doctor marketing to me? Of course! Just as our clients have choices for travel providers, at Kaiser I can select a doctor of my choice.

There is an agent named Debora Ervin from Chattanooga, Tennessee who has also made an impression on me with her database management skills. She has attended a few of my presentations and never fails to send a very unique card to express her appreciation and best wishes. The annual holiday card that she sends is one that is completely personalized to each recipient. This card also includes her picture and her agency's information. I was really surprised and delighted when one of the cards that she sent me had "my" picture on the front. She had created the card from a digital photo that she had taken of me in full costume at a travel conference Halloween party. Debora also included the name of the event, the date and again, on the inside of the card she included her picture in costume, her contact information and another heartfelt note. The company that she uses to create these cards is Send Out Cards – www.sendoutcards.com/appreciatethem. I know how special her efforts have made me feel and I am sure her clients are delighted with her services and caring approach. Do you think that taking the time to touch your clients like this would make a difference in your business? There is no doubt.

KNOW YOUR CLIENT

Imagine yourself in a fine restaurant. Divine table settings, charming atmosphere. Royal Dalton china. Fine crystal stemware. The maître d' offers you the daily special. You lift the silver cloche … UGH!!! It's a pile of *worms*! Grubby – creepy – crawly *WORMS*!!!

The French may have managed to get us to eat snails under the moniker of escargots, but this was beyond ridiculous even if it qualifies as a "low carb/high protein" meal! I would never go back to that restaurant, and I believe you wouldn't either.

How to sell what your customers want and not what you want to

I personally love strawberries and cream. However, when I went on a fishing trip once, I did not get much luck when I baited my hook with a delicious strawberry topped with real Chantilly cream. I found that for some strange reason, *fish prefer worms*! So then I dangled a worm on my hook and within minutes, landed a beautiful 12-pound sea bass.

Those who know me better would realize that this pure dramatization. The only way to get me to touch a sea bass is if it was pan seared and served with a warm lemon dill beurre blanc. But the point I am trying to make is this:

Why not use this common sense when fishing for people?

We tend to talk a lot about what we want to sell. Why on earth would people care about what we want to sell? We need to talk to our customers about what *they* want. When speaking with your customer, you need to stop! Pause and ask yourself, "How do I make this person want what I have to offer?"

I once read an article about when the U.S. Military was trying to sell life insurance to the GIs at war. Most agents had a hard time selling this to the soldiers who figured that their paltry income was better spent on necessities such as beer and cigarettes. Moreover, no one wanted to even consider the prospect of death. Only one agent was able to sell to his quotas and then some. He would have hordes of GIs crowding around begging to sign up. When asked what his secret was, he answered, "I would tell the soldiers that with this insurance, your family will receive a tidy sum of money in the event that you get killed in the line of fire. This pay-out comes out of the military fund. Who do you suppose then; the military will choose to send out on their front lines in time of battle?"

"Travel products have a plethora of features. Success lies in highlighting the ones that our customers are looking for."

Because the name of my agency is Ticket to Travel, many times people will call 411 asking for Ticket Master and inadvertently they will get my phone number. I once had a guy who called looking for tickets to a Jimmy Buffet concert. I told him that I couldn't get him tickets to the concert but I could get him a cruise that would take him to Margaritaville! After laughing and getting into a conversation, I explained that I was a cruise specialist and that there were wonderful cruises that could take him to the land of Jimmy Buffet. It turned out that he and his wife had talked about taking a vacation and I ended up booking a 7-day Caribbean cruise for them.

That, my friends, is called *need-based selling*. For this, follow a three step strategy:

1. *Understand* your product. Every feature, every aspect, every facet
2. *Listen* to your customer. When they are done talking, probe for more information and continue to listen. .
3. *Match* your features to their needs.

Why would customers seeking prestige want to know about the savings of a budget cruise? Paint a Picasso about the formal dinner and shaking hands with the Captain. If your customer is looking for a vacation with her three little ones, do *not* mention the formal dinner. All she will think of is three screaming kids spilling Lobster Bisque on her expensive gown. You will get her attention however, with the soothing spa on deck and the affordable babysitting services.

Our products have a plethora of features. Success lies in highlighting the ones that our customers are looking for.

As for going on a boat for fishing, I am reminded of these words of wisdom: "Give a man a fish and he will eat for a day. Teach a man to fish and he will sit in a boat and drink beer all day." I personally don't care much for beer, but if I were to sell a customized fishing cruise to a bunch of men, I would make sure to sell them one that comes with a cooler full of beer rather than strawberries and Chantilly cream.

Chapter 17 | CLOSING THE SALE

CLOSING THE DEAL

Nothing is more disheartening than to have worked for days, delving out advice, building itineraries and providing every aspect of our services to prospective clients, only to have them not book, or even worse, book their trip elsewhere.

As much as we don't want to admit it, shoppers – often called "tire kickers" – are not a phenomenon exclusive to the travel industry. How many times have you spent the day with a salesperson at a car lot but ended up buying elsewhere? That's where the term "tire kickers" came from. When looking for a special outfit or pair of shoes, do you buy at the first store you visit? Most of us want to make sure that we are getting the best value for our money. The key word here is "value".

Often we get so excited about an opportunity to take care of a new client that we hastily give them all kinds of information: travel brochures, prices, itineraries, web addresses and the like. We forget to add our value to the proposal. Here are a few ways to do that:

> *"Make sure you give clients the opportunity to learn about your services"*

Never try to make a sale before creating a relationship – When I make my first contact with a new client I ask if I can spend a few minutes with them to learn more about their travel preferences. That's the time to start building the personal relationship. It is so important to find out about their past travels and what they liked best and least about the trips. Asking these types of questions shows a genuine interest on your part and opens the lines of communication.

I explain that by knowing their likes and dislikes it will greatly assist me in making the best possible recommendations. This type of information is needed to make sure we don't overwhelm them with too many options. It is our job to sort through the myriad of options and come back with good matches based on the information they provide.

How to keep potential clients from simply "browsing" in your home-based agency

Describe the benefits of your services to clients – Throughout the conversation I weave in the benefits of using my services. I describe of the all of the "extra services" that I provide for my clients, such as complimentary gift baskets, Travel Newsletters, VIP letters to property managers, and so on. I let clients know that I am available to schedule a meeting with them at their convenience, either by phone or in person. They are assured that, should they need anything while they are on their trip, they can feel to call me at any time for assistance.

If they are traveling outside of the United States I offer to keep a copy of their passport in my office and fax a copy to the nearest Embassy for faster replacement if necessary. I also let them know that I will be happy to provide my industry credentials, training, personal experiences, client referrals, and testimonials. I have now given them my value and a reason to book with me.

Learn to sell yourself and your services before you sell pricing and products – If you haven't created this type of "script" about yourself, now's the time to start. If you show a client your value they are less likely to shop around, and even if they do, you may have given them enough reason to come back and book with you.

Offer to meet or beat a price should they find a better price elsewhere.

Act on the assumption that most consumers are not going to buy from you without checking to make sure you are giving them the best deal. Ask clients upfront that if they do find it less expensive elsewhere to give you an opportunity to meet or beat it. Assure them that they can get the best price and your excellent service to boot! This gives them "permission" to return to you guilt-free if they do check around.

My main thought here is to make sure you give the client the opportunity to know about you and your services. If you are getting leads and simply quoting prices, you may not be closing the sales and you risk losing clients to the Internet. You have not given them any reason to want to book with you.

Many times I like to use Nordstrom's as an analogy. It is the same philosophy, people don't go there because of their prices or sales, but because they know that they are going to get great customer service. Now that's value.

Don't be this agent… Create a friendly relationship so that they want to do business with you. Intimidation will only send them to your competition.

EFFORTLESS UPSELLING

Upselling refers to when you help a customer decide to buy related products or upgrades after the final purchase. A car dealer, for example, might inform customers about upholstery protection and undercoating. A shoe salesperson might suggest that when you buy a pair of shoes that you also use some weather-protectant spray. Chain restaurants, such as McDonalds, are the masters of this – have you ever not been offered fries or a drink to go with your burger? And when was the last time you bought an electrical appliance and were not told the benefits of an extended warranty? The travel industry also has lots of "French fries" to offer to go along with clients travel plans, such as, travel insurance, shore excursions, pre and post cruise hotel stays, just to name a few.

Upselling Should Be Easy

Upselling should be practically effortless since most times it's done after the customer has decided to go ahead with the purchase of travel. The hardest part is making the sale and that has already been done. You've already established rapport, identified needs, handled objections, presented benefits, and asked for the order. At this point up selling should be simple by presenting the information in a "by-the-way" assumptive manner.

Assumption Is The Key

You've got to present the products in an assumptive manner as if you already know that the customer will naturally want this. Ask questions, such as, "I would be happy to arrange for your air and transfers to the cruise port. What airport is most convenient for you?" "Would you like the standard travel insurance or the cancel-for-any-reason coverage?" "What day would you like me to arrange for your island tour in Maui?"

To avoid sounding pushy, particularly if the up sell requires some elaboration, ask for the customer's permission to describe it. Begin with a brief benefit and then add something unique about what you're selling.

So What's Keeping You From Upselling?

The simple fact is that most agents simply don't ask. Asking should become a habitual part of your sales process.

Perhaps it's a lack confidence because you haven't been trained on the products or benefits. Do you lack personal experience? *Then get to know your products.* Being knowledgeable is critical to being a total solution provider. Make no mistake, that's what customers are looking for today - ideas, suggestions and solutions.

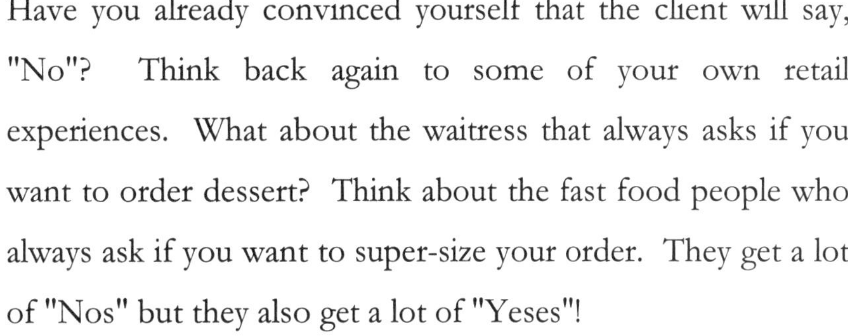

Have you already convinced yourself that the client will say, "No"? Think back again to some of your own retail experiences. What about the waitress that always asks if you want to order dessert? Think about the fast food people who always ask if you want to super-size your order. They get a lot of "Nos" but they also get a lot of "Yeses"!

Maybe you feel you would be trying to sell the customer something that they can't afford or they don't need. Refocus on the client's needs – not yours. It is totally irrelevant whether or not this is something you would purchase. What is relevant is whether it may be a benefit or an enhancement to your client's overall travel experience. This perspective empowers you to up sell effectively.

Try to get out of the mindset of assuming that every customer wants to buy the cheapest product. It is our job as the travel consultant to offer them choices. That is what upselling is all about.

Start with the Relationship

Everything related to successful selling starts with building an initial relationship. Once the customer has made the decision to buy from you, the relationship has been established and they are also ready and willing to listen to you. Once you have established the relationship you now have earned the right to 1) ask questions and 2) make suggestions. Knowing the customer's needs will allow you to make the best recommendations.

These two basic selling strategies focus on helping customers solve their problems. It's much easier to help a customer buy something than it is to sell him something. So what exactly does that mean? Well, it means helping a customer buy is all about helping them figure out what they really need and what will give them the best value. You gain trust by offering good choices and then letting them decide.

Bottom line

The bonus is that these extras can add to your bottom line and be extremely profitable for you. Upselling and suggestive selling is not only a best business practice but it is essential to growth and improved profitability. More importantly, if you sell a customer a travel product without offering them other services to enhance or protect their trip, you may be doing them a disservice.

Chapter 18 | OVERCOMING OBSTACLES AND OBJECTIONS

SELLING TO FRIENDS AND FAMILY

You finally made the decision to go into the travel industry. You want to be a home-based agent, so now you have to think of ways to promote yourself. But to whom and how? Of course, your first thought is "I'll send a letter to all of my friends and relatives." I know that they all travel and now I can let them know that they will now have a friend in the travel business." A piece of cake, right? Not always!

Most of us generally start out by marketing to a so-called "warm market." Your warm market is basically everyone you know: friends, family, colleagues, advisers, teachers, doctor, lawyer, neighbors and other acquaintances.

Reactions will vary once you let those know that you are in the travel business. Close friends and family reaction will probably run from excitement to humoring you. Others who don't know you well may be dismissive or even downright hostile to your approach. Some agents have reported people crossing the street to avoid them when they see them coming! So you may need to develop a thick skin in this business.

And think also about what happens if someone you care about DOES proceed with buying travel from you and everything goes wrong with their trip. Close relationships can be damaged as a result.

All too often these friends and loved ones become our biggest abusers and constantly try to take advantage of our knowledge and time. These sometimes misguided folks flood us with questions and request for discounted travel thinking somehow we must be able to get a "special deal" just for them. After all, we are in the travel business and they are sure that we get secret discounts that are only offered to us. This is such a misconception. In addition, these are usually the most demanding of all clients – calling numerous times asking the same questions over and over, questioning the pricing at every turn, and, worse than anything, always questioning our expertise and advice.

The following is an email I received from an agent about such an incident from a relative that I am sure many of us can relate to.

"Dear Anita – I have an aunt who has repeatedly asked me to look up vacations for her, yet never books. Lately she asked me to do tons of research for a group cruise for her family. Of course I was happy to help, and even suggested other ships and dates that might be better priced. I just got a response back from her indicating that she decided to book with another travel agent who had a better price. To add insult to injury, I found out it was actually on the ship that I had previously suggested! I am at a loss of words of how to respond to her email tactfully, and how to avoid this situation in the future. I am not sure if I am taking this too personal, but to be honest, I am offended and feel used."

I suggested to this agent that if it were me, I would politely tell my aunt how hurt I was that after all the work I had put in that I wasn't given the another opportunity match the price. I would also let her know how much I was looking forward to showing her my services and how I'd planned to make sure that her cruise was a wonderful experience for everyone. I would also add that I was *totally surprised* to find out that she was working with another travel agent all along. (Handing out a little guilt works great as revenge!) Then I would wish her a "Bon Voyage".

The next time a "repeat abuser" contacts you, tell them to shop around for the best deal, then give you a call, and you will be happy to see if you can match or better the price. You need to set boundaries for yourself and your business.

It can be frustrating when after all of your hard work and long hours that you find that you are not taken seriously. It seems that the perception is that you are just dabbling or are in the travel business as a hobby, especially when working from the home. At times even well intended relatives don't really believe you will succeed. Sometimes these are the clients that we just have to "fire".

It also may be a good time to send out a newly revised letter to everyone. Clearly point what this business means to you, what type of business that you are looking for and what you will offer in the way of services and added value. Let people know exactly what type of travel you do and do not offer. For example, since I am not an ARC agency and do not issue airline tickets, in all of my correspondence I always emphasize that I am a "Cruise and Vacation Specialist."

This letter and all forms of correspondence should be well written and sent on professional looking letterhead. If you want people to take you seriously, you will need to project a professional image.

The projection of a professional business will breed more successes and with that will come the well-deserved respectability. Eventually you will be looked at as a serious business owner with the confidence and support of those around you.

LITTLE WHITE LIES

The story goes that, as a child, George Washington chopped down the backyard cherry tree and then admitted the whole sordid affair to his beloved father: "I cannot tell a lie," he is said to have said. "It was I who chopped down your cherry tree."

As much as everyone strives to be as virtuous as our first President, the truth is that people who sell for a living, even well-meaning agents, feel compelled at times to "stretch the truth" on occasion, and here are three likely reasons why:

1. Not familiar with the destination or the product

In many cases, agents are simply too embarrassed to say, "I don't know." It is better to say, "Let me check with my supplier or fellow associates so that I can get back to you with the most current information".

2. Insecure about the relationship with the prospective client

We all want the customers to like us, so sometimes the truth gets bent a bit in an effort to tell the customer what is perceived as what they want to hear. Unless you are good at remembering every detail of conversations, this can become tricky. Remember what the Blue Fairy said to Pinocchio: "A lie keeps growing and growing until it is as plain as the nose on your face."

3. They're only focused on the commission

Some sales people see lying as an easy way to make a quick buck. Sales people who lie for this reason do it because they want the prospect to move too quickly, so that they can make a quick sale, pocket the commission – and move on to the next prospect before the customer can have any second thoughts.

Unfortunately, the vast majority of prospects out there weren't born yesterday or on a turnip truck. 99 times out of 100, they've encountered these lies before, and as a result, they've become conditioned to expect a certain experience from the sales process.

In fact, in many cases, prospects become so good at predicting sales behaviors that they become experts at manipulating the sales process to get exactly what they want – often at the expense of the sales person.

Focus on building trusting relationships and the commissions will come.

Why clients lie to sales people

Of course, when it comes to sales, truth telling (or the lack thereof!) works both ways.

Clients will lie to avoid an annoying sales pitch. They'll lie to protect themselves against overly persistent phone calls and email follow-ups, or to avoid being pressured into making a decision.

LIES CLIENTS TELL AGENTS

"We don't have a vacation in the budget right now."

In reality, although this may be true, they may actually be saying "we have budget money assigned to other things that are considered higher priority."

Your best response: Through questioning and conversation, gather information about where their money is currently being spent. Once you've discovered what's funded and why, reposition your offering and the value it provides so that it becomes higher priority than the budget items that are currently funded.

"I promise to read your quote and the brochure."

Your best response: Stop depending upon brochures except the one that you create on yourself. The only time to start handing out quotes and travel brochures is after you have sold the prospect on you and your services. Continue to build excitement by creating a picture of them on their vacation by describing what they will experience.

"We decided that we don't want a pre-planned vacation. We want to play it by ear and make it an adventure."

Your best response: Why waste your precious time looking for reservations? Why chance ruining your vacation by finding out that hotel rooms, cars, and other activities will not be available? Let me take care of assuring that your time will be spent enjoying a well deserved vacation and not looking for a hotel room. Plus, I will be here to help you should anything go wrong.

"Your competition is much cheaper."

Why do they tell this lie? To get you to drop your prices.

Your best response: If quotes are apple-to-apple you can offer to try to price match. You must also be ready to present the reasons why working with you will bring them higher value than working with your competitor.

"We always get a big discount."

Why they tell this lie: Same as above… they're trying to get you to drop your prices.

Your best response: Stand firm. Demands for discounts, especially at the end of a sales deal are usually just the customer testing to see if they've gotten the "best deal."

NO MORE MR. NICE GUY

As my host agency business grew, I added technology and tools that allowed all of my independent contractors to network and discuss various topics or issues that they face in running their travel business. One topic that seems to come up over and over during our intranet chats is the dilemma of people taking advantage of an agent's expertise and then booking elsewhere. Here's a thread of conversations to help give you the courage to start saying "I'm mad and I'm not going to take this anymore!"

AGENT #1: I don't know if it's because my confidence level as a travel agent is rising, but my partner says that I am getting really "gutsy".

Case in point: One of our friends, who also works on websites, was at the house last night. He and his wife have tons of money and he grabbed some more FREE brochures and asked my opinion about two tour operators. Over the last two years I have been nice to him regarding this issue, but not this time. I remembered that he wanted to charge me $2000.00 to upgrade my website. I told him that I would be happy to answer his questions for $2000.00 since I had already given him free advice twice that he used to successfully book his own travel on Orbitz, even when I had a better deal!

AGENT #2: I asked my dentist if he wanted to clean my teeth for free next time. He asked what I meant by that, and I explained that he and his entire staff asked me for free travel advice ALL THE TIME, but that they never booked with me. To add insult to injury, his dental hygienist mentioned told me that he was going to take the whole office to Oktoberfest. Now, he's going to book with me! I don't think he realized that all along he was asking for free advice all the time. Now he knows!

AGENT #3: I haven't been nice for years. In fact, my own boss became a difficult client by constantly changing his mind, etc. So when he started to do the same thing your dentist did – I fired him as a leisure client! Now he is forbidden to discuss his travel plans or his woes about his messed up reservations with me unless he is going to book with me.

AGENT #4: You've all encouraged me. My dentist recently asked for input on what he should not miss on his trip to New Zealand. He goes with a friend and they do all their own planning. I am going to say something this time – like, maybe we can set up a barter arrangement. You've given me the courage!

AGENT #5: My son's best friend went with his family and two other families to Las Vegas right before Christmas. The next time I saw them I didn't hesitate to say, "The next time you go on a trip I could arrange it for you, and mostly likely get it less expensive as an air and hotel package. Please let me know if I can do that for you." They may or may not do that, but at least I got my point across.

I had another friend talk about booking with Costco at bunko one night. I pulled her aside and said, "Marianne this is what I do for a living, and Costco is my competition." She apologized and said that she had not thought about it.

AGENT #6: The part-owner/part-manager of the restaurant where I eat almost every day (I'm not kidding about that) asked me to look for that vacation rental in Lake Tahoe and a large SUV rental for the drive. I found him a great price for the car, and I had several options for the rental property for him to look over. We had an appointment to meet to choose the home and finalize everything. When I called to confirm, he told me, "Hey, I made the arrangements this morning. I saw something good online, and I just went for it." Suddenly I have lost my appetite for his food.

And here's my favorite:

AGENT # 7: My hairdresser asked for a fly drive to Hawaii (with four other women). I found air for under $400.00 per person and left her a message. I didn't get a call back. When I inquired later, she said, "Oh, we found air for just a bit cheaper." Guess what? I found a new hair dresser... *for just a little bit cheaper.*

[illegible] of the rental property for lunch [illegible] an appointment [illegible] in the [illegible] plates. When [illegible] [illegible] is [illegible]. I saw something good [illegible] building. I [illegible] appears for [illegible] food.

[illegible]

[illegible] for [illegible] \$10.80 per person and [illegible] [illegible] [illegible]

Part IV

FOCUS POWER

Travel Niches

Chapter 19 | BUSINESS TRAVEL

MIXING BUSINESS WITH BUSINESS

If I did a survey I would most likely find that that the majority of agents who are running a home-based travel agency also have other full time jobs. That was certainly the case for me when I started my travel business in 1992.

At that time, I was also was running a very successful business, working as a manufacturer's rep for electronics in the heart of Silicon Valley. As the electronic industry boomed, the competition became fierce, cold calling and cultivating new customers became progressively more difficult.

Agents who work more than one job can use one to bolster the other

Undaunted, I kept pursuing new sales, trying all kinds of new tactics just to get appointments to meet with buyers. I would try anything unusual just to get their attention and peak their interest.

One Halloween, I bought dozens of mini pumpkins, punched a hole in my business card and attached it to the pumpkin with thin black ribbon. I included a note that read, "No tricks, only great service." Another time I put an empty "thank you" balloon in an envelope with a note "Thanking you in advance for considering me as your next new vendor." Corny? Maybe…but surprisingly, I got opportunities that I would have never have gotten using the traditional sales tactics.

Once I had an appointment where I needed to make sure that I got my message across. What I did notice was that these electronics buyers were just plain tired of hearing the same old sales pitch. Times were hectic, and everyone in the Valley was working hard with extremely long hours. It wasn't fun sitting across from a weary buyer who had heard it all. Time and again, I would hear "I'm sorry but we have more than enough vendors at this time."

Even though I sympathized with how overworked many of these people were I was determined that I wasn't going to leave empty handed. It simply took me too long to finally get my foot in the door! I had to think of ways to keep the conversation going, so one day I blurted out "If not printed circuit boards, how about a vacation?" This stopped them dead in their tracks.

I seemed to have the power to take them into a pleasant state of travel possibilities.

When I saw that they were curious, without hesitation I immediately proceeded to tell them about my travel business and my passion for excellent customer service. I would be happy to plan a well-deserved vacation for them, plus take care of all of the smallest details. "I will bring you the brochures, travel guides, videos and anything else you need right here in the comfort of your office and whenever it is convenient for you. Then after we make your reservation, I will deliver your documents and go over all of the particulars to make sure that nothing will be left to chance. After all, you work so hard and this is something that you do not need to worry about. Leave all of the details to me."

What struck me most during these conversations about travel was the transformation of the buyers' personalities as we discussed possible vacations. The tension in their brows started to ease as I mentally transported them into visualizing a relaxing time with friends or family. I seemed to have the power to transport them into a pleasant state of travel possibilities.

This approach worked well for both of my businesses. I ended up planning vacations for many buyers, which gave me an opportunity to demonstrate how I could provide excellent service; and eventually, the travel relationship would lead to new contracts for my rep business.

I realize that not all of you will be able to solicit business at your full time job as I did. However, this can still be done subtlety and skillfully during normal conversations. Remember, the key is not necessarily to sell but to inform. During a conversation, talk about a trip that you planned for someone or mention classes and certification programs that you are participating in. To avoid any problems with management, if prospective clients show interest in your services, tell them that you do not want to take up their time during normal business hours but if they would like to discuss travel further they can feel free to contact you after hours or during the weekend.

How fortunate we are to be selling a commodity that most everyone wants. This was not the case with selling printed circuits boards, that's for sure. The likelihood that I would casually run into a buyer for that product was slim to none. Selling travel is a different story! Almost everyone you meet is a potential new client. What better way to spread the word about your services than through other business opportunities and acquaintances.

SMALL FISH…BIG SPLASH!

Although I do not go out after day-to-day corporate travel bookings, I have expanded my travel business into the lucrative incentive and group meeting segment. To do this, I had to find ways to work my way into this market, even though I knew that I would be competing with large, more established agencies.

SWIM WITH THE BIG FISH

In an effort to expand my home-based agency into this market, I researched and then joined numerous business associations, networking groups, and service organizations. But it takes a lot more work than paying the enrollment dues and hanging a membership plaque on the wall. You must participate and get involved on an ongoing basis. This proved to be the right move, because I am proud to call some of the most powerful people in the area my clients, including the Mayor, president of the chamber of commerce, city manager, and county assessor, as well as numerous presidents and vice presidents of major corporations. You can find many opportunities to socialize with people of influence not only by joining these types of organizations but by volunteering at special community events.

UPSTREAM MARKETING

Try untraditional approaches to marketing, such as this one: I recently put one of my business cards in a jar for a drawing for a free lunch. This restaurant happens to be a favorite meeting place for business people because it is centrally located, with nice ambiance and good food, at a reasonable price. I won a lunch for myself and seven associates. All I had to do was listen to a short presentation by a sales person from a financial planning company.

What the heck? "Why not go?" I thought. So I invited seven of my agents since we were planning on having a lunch meeting anyway. The eight of us went, and while waiting for our lunch to be served, the salesman presented himself and his company, as well as the benefits that he could bring to us should we need his services in the future. He then asked us to fill out a form with our contact information, and gave us his business card and brochure. He then thanked us for our time and told us to enjoy our lunch. What a great marketing idea! It cost him about $10.00 per person to address a targeted market that he would never have had otherwise. You can be sure that I will be giving this approach a try sometime soon!

GIVE THEM THE BAIT

So many times when I ask agents what they do **differently** compared to their competition, they are stumped for a quick answer. If you are going to be networking for new business opportunities, this should be something that rolls out of your mouth in an instant, because that's about all of the time you will have to make your first impression. Figure out what it is that you do best, determine what your target market wants, and explain how you can do that like no one else. Maybe it's serving a particular destination or niche, maybe it's a form of service or maybe it's a way you package and deliver documents. If you still need help, call some of your best clients and ask them why they buy travel from you. Or better yet, ask them why they left their last travel agent to come to you.

USE THE HOOK

> *"Just because you are a small business, you don't need to act like one."*

When approaching companies and business people, you need to have a proposal prepared outlining the benefits of using your services. I also recommend presenting your own personal business portfolio. You can include testimonials, certificates of accreditations, copies of newsletters that you have authored, sample gift certificates used for presenting incentive travel programs, and any other awards you have earned during your travel career. You can put all of this in a half inch binder. I like to slip my contents into page protectors; and as the binder grows, I can add tabs. This also serves as a guide that you can flip through as you are talking, so you won't forget to cover everything you want to convey.

REEL EM IN!

Once you book travel for a client, make sure you live up to all of your hype. This is the time to dazzle travelers with more than promised. Make sure to deliver their documents and include a travel gift from you…everyone enjoys a gift, even a business client.

Booking a high-level executive group is both an honor and a challenge.

On a trip that I booked for an executive business client, I made sure to have the hotel send a note from me to welcome him upon his arrival in the hotel. Knowing that it was important to him that the hotel to have a workout facility, rather than wine, I ordered a plate of fruit and cheese to be delivered each evening with my compliments. Although I knew he had a busy schedule, I made sure to leave him a voice mail to ask if everything was to his satisfaction and, of course, I followed up with a thank you upon his return. All of this attentive customer service and highest level of professionalism gave him enough confidence to annually award me his company's future group trips

Remember, just because you are a small business you don't need to act like one.

GOING THE EXTRA MILE FOR EXECUTIVES

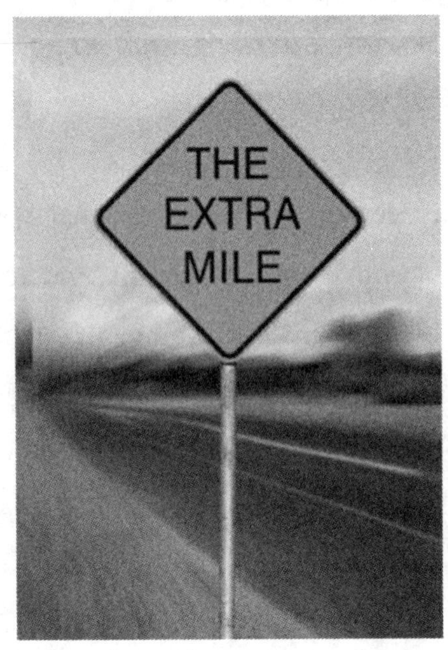

For many years I have had the honor of being the agent selected to book the travel for a very prestigious group of Silicon Valley Executives. This group is an advocacy group that was formed over 30 years ago by David Packard; co-founder of Hewlett-Packard. It was designed to draw on one of the valley's key assets – hundreds of chief executives.

Packard came up with the concept to ask a number of his fellow CEOs to join him in creating a proactive voice for Silicon Valley businesses. The result was the formation of this group, which has successfully tackled some of the toughest challenges facing high-tech employers and their employees. Packard called the first meeting because of the energy crisis and rolling blackouts of the previous summer, but ever since then issues such as housing, transportation and education have continue to be at the top of the group's list.

I won this lucrative travel business from submitting a bid through my local Chamber of Commerce. After securing their first lobbying trip to Washington, D. C., I was awestruck by some of the names of the participants. Who would have ever thought that I would now be able to call these powerful business people "my clients"? I knew that I would have to pull out all of the stops to make sure that everything went perfectly for this group.

Who would have ever thought that I would now be able to call these powerful business people my clients?

After negotiating the contract with the best five-star hotel in Washington, DC, I soon found out that a city such as this one is accustomed to many high-level VIPs and dignitaries. Consequently, no one was surprised when I had special requests that varied all the way from assuring that one executive from the group had special workout equipment to establishing the separate check-in procedures and policies for the Mayor's or other politician's security staff. Not wanting to leave anything to chance, I asked for everything to come back to me in writing. I am sure that they thought that I was a bit paranoid but I wanted to avoid any miscommunication.

Never wanting to miss an opportunity to meet everyone in my groups personally, I came up with an idea to set up a table outside of security at the airport and told the participants to come by the designated meeting place to pick up their travel documents before departure. Because I normally worked through their personal assistants and secretaries, I was aware that this might be a challenge. But my plan went off without a hitch.

Since everyone had e-tickets, I made sure that they each had their individual confirmation numbers for both airlines and the hotel, just in case a problem should arise. Little did they know that I pulled some strings and made special arrangements for a surprise at the airport.

I got up at 3:30AM to go to my neighborhood coffeehouse to pick up a container of fresh brewed coffee and fresh bagels for those "early bird" executives. Inside each "breakfast basket" was my personal brochure and business card. Everyone was thoroughly surprised and impressed with my service and I was thrilled to be able to shake the hands of these high-tech superstars.

Once they arrived at the hotel, I arranged to have a small welcome amenity of chocolate covered strawberries delivered to their room with a personal note from me thanking them for allowing me to take care of their travel plans and wishing them much success with their lobbying trip. Of course, at every communication opportunity, I included my name and personal contact information. Over the years my attention to detail and service has paid off, not only with large commissions, but also with trust, appreciation and loyalty from this group. Not only have I assured their future trips but I have received numerous referrals for other groups similar to this one.

A high-level group such as this requires an agent to know who the players are and what is important when booking a hotel. The first year the hotel needed to be a union hotel. With each year comes a new requirement based on the group's current visions and objectives, along with those of any new participants. This year the group has expanded its environmental awareness, which set a goal for the reduction of greenhouse gases by the Silicon Valley industry. On this last trip I received another glowing report on my services, but I heard back that the hotel, while wonderful, was not quite "green enough." They were very dismayed to see that the lobby had way too many unnecessary lights turned on throughout the hotel. I guess it is also time for Motel 6 to change its long time motto "We'll leave the lights on for you."

Chapter 20 | SELLING HOTELS - FROM ATTRITION TO COMMISSION

AVOIDING HOTEL HAZARDS

A smile flashes across my face when I think of some of my best hotel experiences. I have memories of breakfast in bed, lunch time walks around the grounds, whirlpool Jacuzzi, and spa treatments as and when I please. Where else can you have someone take your luggage, park your car, clean your room and put chocolates on the pillow? Pinch me… I don't want to wake up.

When it comes to planning events for my clients at a hotel, however, I sometimes need to schedule an appointment with my hair dresser prior to the episode because it can become such an ordeal that makes me want to tear my hair out by the roots.

"What makes event planning such a challenge are the myriad factors associated with a hotel stay."

What makes event planning such a challenge are the myriad factors associated with a hotel stay that can make or break a travel or vacation experience. Most of these factors are often outside the realm of your control. There's a lot at stake when planning an event with hotels – chiefly your reputation.

Over the years, I have come to realize that I can't control every circumstance when it comes to event planning. The best course of action is to preempt and prevent any possible mishap to reduce as much as possible the "anything can go wrong" factor.

UNDERSTAND THE VARIOUS HOTEL BRANDS

There are so many hotel brands out there it's sometimes hard to differentiate one from the other. The Diamond rating no longer tells you much about a hotel. Fairmont, Four Seasons and Ritz Carlton offer class, luxury and distinctive surroundings. Westin, Hyatt and Marriott boast of contemporary surroundings and clean, efficient service. The W and Park Hyatt are all about boutique experiences and niche marketing. These are all four-diamond properties. It's important to understand the brand of hotel that you are dealing with, what client niche is best served and which client can best be matched to what's offered.

UNDERSTAND YOUR TARGET AUDIENCE

Understand the demographic to which your clients belong. Ask the questions – are they predominantly women or men? What is the age group? Are any kids or spouses traveling? This will help you match them with the appropriate property.

Can you imagine the dumbfounded look on the middle-aged conservative traveling with his wife in a lobby the W adorned with New Age art, set to music selections ranging from hypnotic trance to lounge techno? Enterprising young business-minded people (a.k.a. workaholics) are going to love the Hyatt rooms with their four- plug sockets on oversized work desks, flat-screen plasma TV's and IPod docking stations. But do you think Grandma and Grandpa looking to spend time with their grandkids are going to be impressed with that?

UNDERSTAND THE LOGISTICS OF A HOTEL

Sometimes it's not the hotel per se, but logistics around the hotel that could make or break the stay. How far is the hotel from the airport? What good is it if you got the client a fantastic rate on the hotel room, if they have to pay $100.00 in taxi fare to get to and from the place? If your clients are driving in, find out what the parking limitations are, and more importantly, what the cost of parking is at the hotel. For example, you can expect to pay up to $60.00 per night to park your car in San Francisco.

UNDERSTAND THE HOTEL LOCATION

If you're booking a "Bride's Night Out," what good is it to have 25 sports bars within walking distance of the hotel? For that Engineer's symposium, do you really think they care if you housed them three doors down from Macy's, Prada or the 24-hour spa center?

In my early days as an agent, I once booked accommodations for some California clients attending a conference in Chicago. The hotel had a better price than the convention hotel and boasted "walking distance" from the Convention center where the meetings were held. Not really an issue, right? Think again. The conference took place at the end of January and Californians don't really know how to dress warm. That was the one aspect which dampened their experience of an otherwise flawless trip.

Working with hotels and planning events are hard tasks. It takes years of experience and intimate knowledge of hotels to get it right. It can be the cause of a lot of stress and fatigue, but you can be sure that it is worth it. A successfully planned event will allow you to build a strong bond with your client – a bond that will bring you more repeat business, more business opportunities and of course, more profit.

HOTEL CONTRACTS

When running a home-based business, you will more than likely enter into a number of types of contracts or agreements, including verbal and contractual. Both can create legal and financial problems for you unless you understand all of the ramifications and responsibilities.

When securing group space, for example, it is common to have a formal agreement between the hotel and the client. In most cases, since you will be representing your clients, you [your agency] will be the responsible party on the contract and so it is important to realize that these are legal and binding agreements so it is imperative that you understand each and every part of the contract before signing. If you are working through a host agency, it is more than likely that you will not have the authority to sign a contract on their behalf.

EVERYTHING IS NEGOTIABLE

Everything is negotiable when you're working with hotels and resorts.

When it comes to working with hotel contracts, the biggest lesson that I have learned is that just about everything is negotiable, from commission to attrition.

Negotiating will frequently involve a series of inquiries and conversations between the hotel, yourself and your client before an agreement can be reached. This process may take several days to several weeks. The bottom line in negotiating is that the hotel needs to make a profit on the business and, your client must be assured that they are paying a reasonable price, and you should end up making equitable commission for servicing the group.

To put yourself in the best negotiating position, first check competitive pricing, including online sources, as well as the hotel's website to make sure you are being offered the best group rate. Next, you should request a clause in the contract that if the hotel does lower their rates to guests during the meeting dates, they will offer those same rates to your group. While a hotel may not be willing to provide the lowest rare offered, it may agree to the lowest group rate, as well as to the stipulations that it will not advertise a lower rate. You should also know that hotels that sell rooms to hotel-room wholesale Web sites, such as Priceline or Expedia, cannot control the prices offered via those Web sites once they have sold the rooms to the site.

Here are some of the things that you can negotiate with hotels and resorts:

- **Net or commissionable rates** – Several contracts that I have received came in at the room rate that I wanted, but they were net rates. I was able to go back to the hotel and negotiate a commission without raising the rate.
- **Complimentary rooms –** These are typically offered by the hotel on a "one for 50" basis – in other words, the 51st room is free. This is also negotiable but you need to be specific on how this will be calculated. It is to your advantage to have

complimentary rooms calculated on a cumulative basis. That is, you should receive each complimentary room as the room pickup increases, calculated by adding all rooms booked by attendees for pre-conference, conference, and post-conference dates. Hotels may also offer complimentary or discounted rooms for staff.

- **Room upgrades –** Suites, room upgrades for VIP's, complimentary cocktail receptions or coffee breaks can also be negotiated. For one of my groups, I actually negotiated to have the hotel include a welcome amenity for each room on my behalf, as well as private check-in.

- **Family plans –** A family plan indicates the hotel's policy on charges for children staying with parents. Many hotels offer no charge for children less than 18 years of age when they stay in their parent's room. Make sure this is in the contract if you feel that there may be families in your group.

- **Pre-and post- rates –** Negotiate pre-conference and post-conference rates for guests who want to come in before and after your main room block dates. This can assist your group in meeting the attrition requirements (see below).

- **Meeting rooms –** Meeting-room rental charges are negotiable, and can be waived, especially if you are securing a large number of rooms at the hotel.

- **Attrition fees –** Think of attrition fees as insurance for the hotel that you will commit to paying for a specific number of rooms within your contracted block of rooms. Attrition fees ensure that the group's business will produce a specified minimum of revenue – either by using the rooms or by paying the difference between the number of rooms that were contracted to be used and the number of rooms that were actually used. The percentage of attrition (reduction from contracted number) will be stated in your contract. Typical attrition policy is 10%. This means you can reduce your group space by no more than 10% without penalties. For example, if you have 100 rooms blocked, 90 would meet your commitment, but you end up with only booking 85 rooms, your group would be responsible for paying for the five rooms, even though they were not used.

Don't be timid about asking for adjustments and other concessions, as hotels will expect negotiations. To be successful you must negotiate from a position of having all of your facts in hand beforehand.

Chapter 21 | GROUP TRAVEL

THE DYNAMICS OF GROUPS

What you need to know to successfully sell group travel

How do you go from being a travel agent who handles only airfare and hotel accommodations to becoming a group travel coordinator? This transition happens when you start handling a larger percentage of other parts of the event, such as meal functions, meeting space, activities, etc.

Although group travel can be very lucrative, there are some duties and financial responsibilities that you will want to consider before making the crossover. Group travel brings people together for a common purpose, and meeting and travel planners work to ensure that this purpose is achieved seamlessly. What your group leader will seek from you will be a well-planned itinerary along with the assurance that you will be able to offer each individual within the group personal attention and guidance.

Creativity, as well as marketing and public relations experience, will work greatly to your advantage. You should also have a solid handle on the following skills: verbal and written communication, organization and time management, and negotiation and budget management. Following are specific tips for coordinating groups.

Be ready to provide promotional assistance – You may be requested to assist with creating flyers in both print form and email format. In addition, be available for questions about the trip at promotional meetings or events.

Prepare a registration website – The group may require you to have online registration capabilities. If this is added to your website, the cost to modify your site to accept online guest registration should be factored into the overall fees. If the registration is on the client's site, request that automatic responses come to you.

Understand the contracts you sign – You will be required to understand any legal contracts and terminology. Don't be afraid to ask questions and get explanations in writing of any terminology or clauses that you don't fully understand.

Understand room block attrition clauses – This is the difference between the actual number of sleeping rooms picked up and the number agreed to in the terms of the hotel's contract. Usually there's an allowable shortfall of around 10% before damages are assessed. For example, if there are 100 in the room block, the group will be liable for 90 rooms. Typically a hotel will work with you, but hold you to the contract unless they can resell the rooms. This needs to be explained carefully to your group. The hotel also should agree not to offer special promotional rates or weekend packages that are less than the contracted rate during the meeting period unless such special rates apply to all rooms within the organization's room block.

Negotiate the best hotel at the best rate – Remember to ask about the hotel's peak, off-peak and shoulder seasons, as well as which days of the week would be preferable to book business. If your group's dates are flexible, you may be able to shift to a more attractive rate. Schedule your negotiations early, ideally six months or more in advance. The larger the group, the more time is needed.

Seek any concessions up front in the contract. Such concessions are ways to reduce the cost to your group. For example, you can ask for complimentary meeting space if you're able to book 85 or 90 percent of the room block. You can get coffee at cost or 10 % off all food and beverage; or one complimentary room for every 40 booked (the standard in most contracts is one room from every 50).

Be prepared for changes – As the contractual deadlines approach, groups can quickly go into panic mode. With one of my recent groups, the clients had me going in a million directions a week before the trip's departure. The phone calls started flooding in, "Can you please ask for an extension on the cut-off date for my group?" "Can we make name changes?" I was going crazy, but then in the end they had me add an additional 15 rooms because the participants waited until the last minute. Luckily the hotel was able to accommodate them.

Find out about meeting planner programs – In some cases, you may qualify to earn reward points for booking your group with a particular hotel chain. It will be up to you to inquire about any programs and what you will need to do to qualify your group's stay. I once earned a $1,000 American Express gift card merely by asking about any current offers for meeting planners.

GROUP TRAVEL ...*FREE TRAVEL!*

Don't you get tired of everyone wanting the cheapest deals? The next time clients asks for that bargain trip, let them know that you can arrange free travel for them to any destination or cruise of their choice. Who doesn't want to travel for FREE? This is especially enticing to those who work, play or associate with others who also love to travel. Your conversation could continue something like this: "Have you ever thought of escorting a tour or going on a cruise with a group of friends or family members? The program is pretty simple...just

How to entice great group leaders and sell more groups

determine where **YOU** would like to go and start recruiting. Before you know it you will have a **FREE** trip!"

EXPLAIN HOW THE "TRAVEL FOR FREE" PROGRAM WORKS

After selecting the date and destination, make sure that the group leader understands the contractual ramifications for deposits, final payments, cancellation clauses, etc., from the particular cruise line or tour operator. I usually request that the agreement be sent to me from the supplier in a format that I can modify to then become a formal agreement to be between myself and the group leader.

Add to the agreement the terms for their free travel. For example, if you recruit 15 people to go on the same cruise, you will get a FREE BERTH. If you get 16 couples in a group, you will get a FREE CABIN. It's important that they know that these are numbers that must be met in order for them to earn their free travel. Make it clear that the will be responsible for taxes or other fees. They should also agree that they will still participate on the trip and be responsible for their own payment for travel arrangements should the group numbers not materialize. Ask for a signature as acceptance of the agreement after you have covered all of the important facts and have reviewed the terms and conditions.

GIVE YOUR GROUP LEADER THE RIGHT TOOLS

Create and print specific flyers that the leader can mail or distribute to potential group participants. Many times I have been able to get co-op or full marketing assistance from the tour operator or cruise line to cover the cost of printing. There have been some suppliers who have had their in-house graphics department create a customized flyer or brochure that included my logo and contact information. Don't be afraid to ask for this type of funding or assistance from your preferred suppliers.

I like to create a complete informational binder for my group leader that contains all of the pertinent details about the trip. Having this data at their fingertips allows them to answer any questions from potential participants, thus reducing the calls or emails that would normally come to you. The binder will include a copy of the flyer, the complete itinerary, pre- and post-opportunities, frequently asked questions with answers, costs per passenger, double and triple occupancy rates, airline schedules or options, excursions, pertinent informational pages cut from brochures, packing tips, weather, etc.

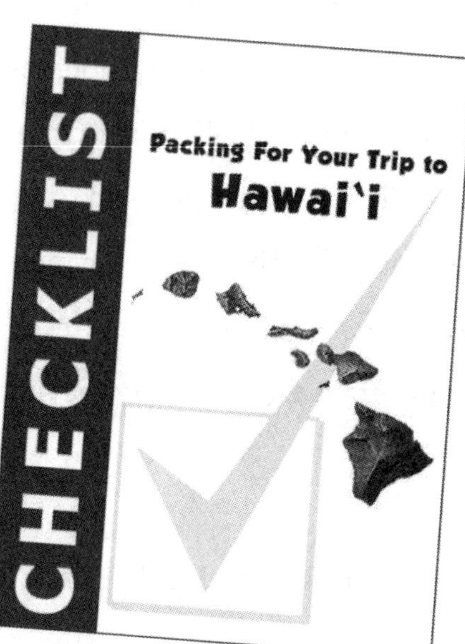

PREPARE YOUR GROUP

Send out regular notices on updates or important information regarding the trip. There should be first time cruiser information, check lists for packing, baggage limitations, citizenship requirements, etc. In addition to the pertinent information regarding security and travel arrangements, it's important to keep the group enticed and excited. Send out information regarding the destinations that they will be visiting and highlight special attractions and points of interest. Make yourself the expert and give them personal insights and recommendations for excursions, shopping and dining.

As imperative as it is to have a good relationship with the group leader, it is important for the group's success that you meet with the entire group whenever possible. This not only gives you an opportunity to give firsthand information and knowledge, it gives you a chance to inadvertently introduce yourself and your services to each member. This is an excellent way to secure future individual travel business.

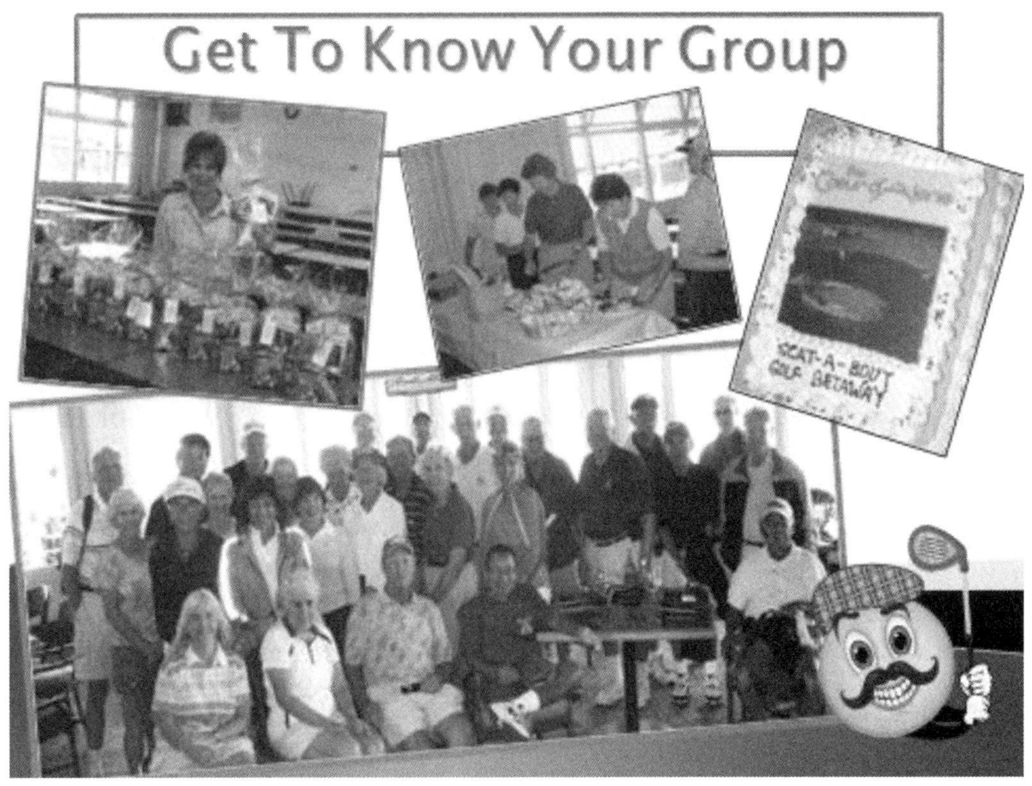

For example, one of my group leaders is a golf pro, and before any golf getaway we meet in one of the class rooms at a campus where he teaches. I provide a lunch that includes sandwiches, chips and sodas. I bring a cake for desert which has a picture of the golf course on the top. Most large bakeries can now do this type of **photo cake** where they will scan a picture onto edible frosting sheets. The bakery can scan anything from post cards, pictures of ships from brochures and your personal photos of a destination. Nurture your groups in this manner and you will surely get your "Piece of the Cake" in the future!

ESCORT SERVICE…GOING WITH THE GROUP

I happen to love escorting groups but it's certainly not for everybody. You really have to like people and responsibility, and be willing to do a lot of hand-holding. How you escort a group that is critical to developing future repeat groups as well as growing your individual business.

As an escort, you must start your job months before the group ever leaves, at the conception of the group, and it doesn't stop until everyone returns home. If the group is booked more than a year out, start with monthly communication such as packing tips, local customs and destination highlights. As the trip gets closer you can start sending weekly messages regarding information on foreign money exchange outlets, weather updates, reminders to check airline schedules and seat assignments, etc.

To foster group camaraderie make sure to arrange a "Welcome Cocktail Party or Group Get Together" at the start of the trip. This party also is a good time to give everyone a welcome gift from you. When choosing a group gift, it is best to give something that you will be assured everyone will use throughout the trip. For example, a passport holder that hangs around the neck can also double as a name badge. T-shirts or hats that have the group's name on them, such a Smith Family Reunion or ABC Realty Sales Conference, can help you bring more unity to the group. I try to build the cost of this party into the trip, along with the cost for any giveaways and prizes. For marketing purposes, also make sure that any item you give away also bears your company name and logo.

Hold periodical get-togethers that are fun and informative. For instance, I have a women's travel group consisting of 26 ladies whom I took on a Mediterranean cruise. Before our departure I put together 3 separate events over several months. On one night I arranged a packing demonstration at popular women's clothing store. On another night we had a no-host dinner at a local Mediterranean restaurant. On yet another day we met at an IMAX theatre to see the movie "Greece: Secrets of the Past." When we went on the cruise, I provided each of the ladies with a copy of the beautiful Greek music from the movie as a fun bonus gift.

It's important to get to know as much as possible about the participants of your group in advance. I like to send everyone in the group a bio sheet which asks where they have traveled before, as well as what they like and don't like to do. The questionnaire also asks for passport information, which gives me their age without having to directly ask for it. It also inquires about medical conditions and food allergies, which can be critical information during a trip.

If geographical diversity of the group makes it difficult to get together, create online communication, such as a Yahoo Group email site where participants can start a dialog with each other. If there are optional tours available, I offer to put together an Excel spreadsheet so that the group can see who is going on which excursions.

Get to know as much about the participants of your group in advance.

If you offer to match singles for the group, find ways to let the roommates connect in advance so that when the trip leaves they are not strangers meeting or talking for the first time. Encourage them to exchange email messages, have phone conversations or if possible meet in person in advance of the trip. This may hedge off any difficult or uncomfortable situations during the trip when it may be too late that they find that they are totally incompatible.

In preparation for the trip, I create customized pre-printed postcard size invitations using a Microsoft Publisher template. I can then leave these under doors to remind the participants of special group events. For an example, it may say something like "Meet us at the Stratosphere Lounge at 7:30PM for a welcome no-host cocktail party".

Escorting a group can be extremely rewarding but also demanding.

I find escorting a group to be extremely rewarding, as well as demanding. Indeed, it is important to remind yourself that this is your job and not your vacation. You should be willing to give your participants access to your cell phone and room number should anything arise that needs your assistance. You must be ready and prepared to handle all of the smallest details as well as learn the crisis management techniques involved with leading groups such as finding lost luggage, helping people who are ill, and dealing with accommodation problems. This doesn't mean that you can't enjoy the trip and have fun yourself, but the guest's comfort and enjoyment should be your number one priority.

BIRDS OF A FEATHER

As the old saying goes, "Birds of a feather flock together" and so goes the group travel concept

Whether people are interested in Harley-Davidsons, jazz or scrapbooking, there is a trend toward organizing a trip around a common interest.

Hobbyists

I once put together a group cruise for nearly 100 scrapbookers. The key to my success with this group was to find the right scrapbook store to partner with. I searched for a store that already had a large database of customers. For marketing purposes, it was also important that they held regular scrapbooking sessions and events at the store. It was then a matter of putting together mutual marketing plans, time lines and estimated expenses, which we built into the price of the cruise.

Birds of a Feather
Flock Together

We sent out regular announcements to both of our databases, held special "Cruise Night" events to answer questions and take reservations, and hosted other events to keep everyone exciting and informed. As an example, I realized that packing would be a challenge since the participants would need to take a lot of their scrapbooking supplies on the cruise, so I arranged for an evening at popular women's clothing store that did packing demonstrations to show how you could pack for a one week cruise in a small carry-on bag. The clothing store was so eager to have this type of exposure to a new group of shoppers they even provided the refreshments and snacks for the event. A week before the cruise we held a "Get organized for the cruise" event. The scrapbook store employees offered assistance as well as a discount on any products that they may need to bring. The cruise was a huge success taking months of planning, work and close coordination with both the scrapbook store and with the cruise line.

Group Honeymoons

When I have honeymoon clients interested in a cruise, I always suggest that they should think about inviting family and friends along on their honeymoon. After they get over the initial shock of my suggestion, I remind them that unless they are going to a secluded island somewhere that more than likely they will be traveling in the company of others. Then why not let it be friends and family? Couples who have taken my suggestion tell me that it was the best way to keep the wedding party going and yet they still had plenty of private romantic time together as well.

Family & Friends

Traveling with groups of family members and friends can be a fun and very memorable event. Whether your clients are looking for a cruise, tour or vacation package, let them know that you can handle their reservation from start to finish ensuring that everything goes just right.

To get started, ask the group leader to provide you with a list of family members that they would like to invite. The best way to get everyone the information is to email or mail an itinerary to everyone that is invited. This can be done by the group leader, or if they are willing to provide the database, offer to do this for them. Inform them of the date, destination, cost and any other relevant information. Make sure to put an RSVP date. You may also just want to send out a "Save the Date" email to let people know that the group is in the works even before the main details are all settled.

Religious Groups

When initially contacting a religious organization, you will need to emphasize to the decision-maker that group travel is great way to develop a closer community among their members. Visiting religious sites enhances one's faith and provides a wonderful opportunity to experience historical destinations.

> *It is estimated that more than 48,000 churches across American participate in organized group travel!*

It must be established up front who will be escorting the trip so that you can build their travel expenses into the program. For example, a Christian group that we once promoted required that the travel expenses be covered for the Pastor, his wife and the church's administrative assistant. We worked with a supplier who built their travel expenses into the per-person cost.

Here is a great statistic: It is estimated that more than 48,000 churches across America participate in organized group travel!

Incentive Groups

What is the best way to promote bigger sales and higher productivity? Travel rewards, of course! More and more companies understand the benefits of travel rewards that are based on certain performance levels. This can be done on an individual basis but group rewards have an even larger payoff. One company that I worked with held a sales contest and took all of their top performers on a cruise to Mexico. Once I explained that included in their price was the use of meeting rooms and audio-visual equipment, they found it the perfect way to mix business with pleasure!

SELLING CRUISES FOR A CAUSE

Once a month I join a Saturday Chat with agents across the states. We pick a specific topic and brainstorm ideas on how to build our businesses. One month's topic was "How to sell successful fundraising cruises," and the conversation was led by agents, Keith and Martha Powell.

Martha's sincere love for the world of travel led her to the decision to step back into the industry to enable her to focus on fundraising cruises for non-profits. A cancer survivor herself and advocate for patients and families, Martha says "What better way than to serve this community than to fund raise and benefit organizations that serve people whose lives have been touched by cancer?"

Keith joined his wife to come up for a way to take fundraising, or as they like to call it "FUN Raising" to the sea. For every cruise they sell, a portion will be donated back to the organizations that are dear to Martha's heart. This is the first key to success – find an association that you have a passion for and then get involved. Martha has been a longtime supporter and volunteer for PLTC, "People Living Through Cancer." So when the Powells approached the organization with the idea of a fund-raising cruise there already was a feeling of trust.

In order to choose the right cruise product it will be necessary to look at the organization's mission statement to understand their charter as well as their demographics, such as age of participants, economic situations, etc. Look for milestones or anniversaries for the group and build your presentation around this – "Sail with XXXX Charity celebrating our 20th Anniversary."

When approaching an organization it is important to meet with the decision-maker or board of directors. Have a business plan that outlines the benefits:

- Bring in needed funds with minimum effort on your part
- Participants will enjoy a fun vacation while supporting a worthwhile cause
- Press releases and advertising will bring more recognition to the organization and charity
- Friends and family tend to vacation together so you gain access to potential new contributors
- Unique opportunity to spend quality time with contributors, volunteers and supporters

- Opportunity to create an annual event – promotes fellowship and loyalty among participants
- There will be different options to raise funds, such as marking up the group rate or by taking the value of the earned free berths as the contribution.

Point out the benefits of a cruise, which will be nearly all-inclusive and will be much easier than putting on a marathon, banquet dinner or auction, which can be time and energy consuming for their staff. Not to mention, with a cruise, they won't be faced with the large upfront costs that these other types of events require.

An additional way to raise funds would be for the organization to hold a raffle for a cabin on the same cruise. The cost for the free cruise could either be built into group pricing or by utilizing earned free space from the group. Participants would still be encouraged to book their cabin with the caveat that their deposit would be refunded if they win the raffle.

Select a cruise that has a low price point, such as a soft sailing, which will allow for a larger mark up and profit margin. Also look for a sailing that has a greater amount of amenity points to use for group cocktail parties, bonus commissions, etc. To keep the group leaders motivated, find out what destinations that they want to visit. Once you have selected the cruise line, itinerary and date, go to your local sales rep and see what the cruise line can do to match funds, offer co-op assistance and add extra amenity points for the group sailing.

The Powell's were delighted when they handed over a $5000.00 check to their charity after their first FUNraising cruise. In addition to benefiting the organization they also arrange for speakers and onboard events that make their cruises unique and appealing to everyone in the cancer survivorship community. Some other tips they offer are:

- Have a written plan and set weekly and monthly goals
- Stay active within your group and do regular presentations
- Get back to inquiries within 24 hours
- Send Thank You letters with each deposit

- Have separate business cards printed just for the group cruise
- Be ready to take bookings for the next cruise while you are on the current cruise

Challenge yourself to reach out to your community and find a charity that you can help benefit by organizing a fundraising cruise. Remember that you are not the "non-profit" in the proposal and that there is enough money to be earned for both you and the cause.

LEADER OF THE PACK

The ultimate outcome for selling groups is not only the initial higher revenue that it will generate, but to get the repeat business, whether it is a group that repeats every year or individual travelers. Selling a group is only the first step to assure that you end up with the results that you want. Below I have outlined what it takes to nurture a group booking, from the inception to the welcome home.

ANITA'S MULTI-STEP PROGRAM TO KEEP YOUR GROUP CRUISE BUSINESS SAILING ALONG

Selling groups is an ideal way to generate repeat business – but you have to do it right!

Once I have group space confirmed for a cruise, for example, I create a binder complete with all of vital information regarding all pertinent aspects of the cruise that includes a complete inventory of staterooms that have been allocated by category. As staterooms are assigned, I log them in so that I can readily see what is still available or what needs to be added. I record when deposits are due and when group space will be recalled, and I also add these important dates to my electronic calendar in Outlook for automatic reminders. A duplicate binder, minus any commission or proprietary agency information, is created for the group leader or pied-piper. With this indexed information at their fingertips, they will then be equipped to answer most questions that arise and eliminate unnecessary calls and emails. Such information includes:

- Complete cruise itinerary, including information on each of the ports
- Ship facts, highlights, and activities for all ages
- Driving directions to the pier, or airport transfer information
- Suggested times to schedule arrival and departure flights
- Pre- and post-cruise options
- Complete description of cabin categories, including availability, square footage and view options.
- Pricing for singles, and first, second, third, and fourth person per category.
- Brochure, deck plans and cabin layouts
- Complete list of what is and isn't included in the price.

- Insurance options
- Proof of citizenship requirements
- Gratuity guidelines
- A complete list of the most frequently asked questions, which includes concerns about anything from seasickness to what to wear.

I also provide the group leader with a supply of customized registration forms. Each guest is required to fill out an individual registration. Information required includes:

- Legal name, type of proof-of-citizenship, date of birth, address, phone numbers and email address.
- Name(s) of roommate(s).
- Emergency contact information.
- Special needs, medical conditions, and if they will be celebrating any special occasions.
- A check box to indicate which category they want. I include the per-person pricing next to the check box so that there is no misunderstanding. (Make sure to let them know if bedding for the 3rd and 4th person is Pullman style.)
- A place to indicate if this is their first cruise. If so, I will send them my "First Time Cruiser Guide." If they have cruised before, I ask how many times and for their past passenger numbers.
- Clearly state deposit and final payment amounts along with due dates plus all cancellation and penalty rules.
- Form of payment and a box to check to authorize automatic use of their credit card for the final payment.

- They must either decline or request further information and pricing for travel insurance.

In addition, everyone must attest via a signature that they have read the terms, conditions and disclaimers on the registration form. (When you have a third-party group leader or pied-piper providing information to participants, this is extremely important.) I then record all of the information gathered into an Excel database for quick future reference. It's important to keep the group excited so I send tips and news on the cruise periodically. If the participants are local, I will arrange for a coffee-and-dessert meeting, so that I can personally give everyone their documents. This gives me an opportunity to meet everyone and to answer any questions. For a fun dessert idea, take a picture of the ship from a brochure to a bakery who can copy it on the top of the cake. Have them write "Bon Voyage" to the group on it.

> *"The ultimate outcome of selling groups is not just higher revenue but repeat business."*

I also put together a packet of letters and reminders for the group leader to distribute to the group participants on board. There will be a "Welcome Aboard" letter on my behalf wishing them a "Bon Voyage." If I have provided a bottle of wine or gift for the cabin, I will include a note saying "I hope that they enjoy the wine." (On a past group cruise, the cruise line did not include my agency's name on the gift card and only that it was from "your travel representative", which I felt was a bit ambiguous. I now include this in my welcome aboard note so that the clients know that the amenity actually came from me.) Also included in the packet will also be included pre-printed postcards that I create in a Microsoft Publisher file which will remind them of the time and location for any special events such the group cocktail party or portraits.

Finally, place a welcome home call to each participant. I find that this is so much more personable than email or letter. As for the group leader, I invite him or her out to lunch or dinner for a follow up meeting on the results of the cruise. That's also a great time to initiate the planning process for group's next cruise.

Chapter 22 | LUXURY TRAVEL

The Rich Get Richer…AND SO CAN YOU!

I am a very curious person by nature, so when I decided to make one of my main business goals to sell luxury travel to wealthy individuals, I wanted to find out what makes these type of people tick. Where do millionaires and affluent individuals spend their money? I wanted to know exactly how they allocated their wealth and what was important to them and their lifestyle. What are their expectations? What I discovered was, for the most part, wealthy people spend much the same way as the rest of us, just more of it and on much nicer things.

Here is some interesting research that was done on owners of Private Jets:

- The owners of private jets have an average annual income of $9.2 million and a net worth of $89.3 million.
- The average age is 57 years old and 70% of them are men.
- $542,000 a year is spent on home improvements.
- Automobile purchases and expenses total $226,000 per year
- $117,000 on clothes and a whopping $248,000 a year on jewelry
- The average jet setter spends nearly $30,000 per year on alcohol.
- They have more than two principal residences worth at least $2 million each.

- They crave "experiential travel," which includes guided tours, such as photographic safaris, or hikes to Machu Picchu, or eco-tours to the Brazilian rainforest, or kayaking in Baja California during the gray whale migration. For these experiences, jet setters spend an average of $98,000 per year.
- Events and stays at hotels and resorts $224,000 a year.
- The average jet setter spends $107,000 a year at spas around the world.

Understanding the dynamics and desires of the luxury customer.

For most of us it is hard to comprehend spending this kind of money but if this is the market you are after, you have to get accustomed to understand the dynamics of their lifestyles and what qualifications you will need to attract them to do business with you.

It turns out that just 34% of jet owners open their own mail and only 19% pay their own bills. The advantage here is that the last thing that they want to deal with is the complex details of planning a vacation. These types of people seek out serious professional help.

The good news is that you can bet that they won't be spending hours on the internet looking for the next best deal.

KEY MISTAKES TO AVOID

Don't be afraid to make money. Get comfortable with the amount of money that a luxury client spends. If luxury is what they're after, be confident they know what it will cost.

Not all luxury clients are "obvious" in their lifestyle. I remember once meeting a client for lunch and it struck me odd that there was this older man waiting at the entrance as he was dressed in extremely worn overalls and it did not look like he was a likely patron. My first thought was that he may be looking for a hand out. Once seated inside the older man walked in and you would have thought that a rock star just entered. It turned out that he was "Mr. Olson" of Olson's Cherries, which was once the largest cherry orchard in Silicon Valley. In fact, he owned the land that the swanky restaurant was built on. Good lesson learned!

WHAT ARE THE EXPECTATIONS IN THIS MARKET?

First and foremost these customers will expect extraordinary service. Being aware of this, I re-engineered my business and marketing slogan to reflect that of a "Vacation Concierge." However, I had to be able to stand behind that claim with every new client, knowing that I most likely would only get one opportunity to prove my worth.

I remember once arranging for a limousine to take a new wealthy client to the airport. Nervous that the limo wouldn't show up, I arranged to also be at their residence under the guise of wishing her a "Bon Voyage." As it turned out, the limo was on time and the client was very happy to see me as well.

In fact, I was shocked when she presented me with a bouquet of flowers. I thought to myself "How sweet and thoughtful." Then she went back in the house and came out with a bag of groceries. Her third trip out produced a bowl of live goldfish and a request to take the whole lot to her daughter's house. I remember laughing all the way to the daughter's as the water was splashing out of the goldfish bowl. I just kept saying, "Please don't die, please don't die!"

> *"Get comfortable with the amount of money that a luxury client spends."*

This story happened more than six years ago and the client is still loyal to me. She continues to trust me to handle all of her travel arrangements, as well as her goldfish.

KEEPING UP WITH THE JONESES

I normally do not watch a lot of television, but one day as I was flipping through the channels, I found one of the cable channels airing a marathon of episodes of the reality show "The Real Housewives of Orange County." In the opening segment, as the theme music is playing, the cameras are showing a guard opening the gates to allow the viewers inside to see a glimpse of the luxurious homes in this exclusive area of Southern California. The next scene panned quickly to several vignettes of the private lives of the featured families that live inside the gates. It was during this opening scene that the announcer read aloud what is scrolling across the screen… **"There are 30 million people living behind gated communities in the United States."** Well, that certainly grabbed my attention and I ended up watching several of the episodes in the marathon.

How to capitalize emerging affluence of America's gated communities.

As I soon found out, "The Real Housewives of Orange County" follows five sophisticated women and their families who lead glamorous lives in a picturesque gated community where the average home has a $1.6 million price tag and residents include CEOs and retired professional athletes. It soon becomes obvious that the Orange County "housewives" are used to the good life and will do everything they can to hang on to it.

In one episode, Lauri, one of the housewives, is shown enjoying her vacation with millionaire fiancé George in beautiful St. Tropez. In another episode, one of the other housewives Vicki, starts preparing for an upcoming and long overdue vacation. I was intrigued as I watched Vicki drive her family, friends and co-workers insane as she prepped for a relaxing two-week cruise to Europe. Her blood pressure reached an all-time high as she tried to figure out how to let go of her business for two whole weeks. But equally important to her was to make sure that their cruise was on the best cruise line and she had the most luxurious staterooms for her and her family.

Vicki is a savvy, successful business woman who states in one of the episodes that her lifestyle **is** the "Joneses" and other people want to be just like her. "Keeping up with the Joneses" is a popular catchphrase that refers to the desire to be seen as being as good as someone's neighbors by comparing other's social stature and lifestyle or the accumulation of material goods and money. This phrase most likely came about originally because of the fact that "Jones" is a very common name, implying a majority of people. To some people not "keeping up with the Joneses" is perceived as failing or being inferior.

This same scenario happened with one of my own "gated community" clients. She was in charge of planning a family reunion cruise. I found it interesting that a large number of the other family members had very tight budgets and wanted inside cabins or lowest-priced ocean- staterooms and only a few bought verandahs. However, it was paramount to my client to have the very best stateroom on the ship. Her words to me were "Do whatever you need to do to get us the Presidential Suite." Price was not an issue and it became obvious during our conversations that it was very important that she be able to show her family the financial status and spending ability that she had achieved.

I have found that inside these gated communities there is a surprisingly large segment of young affluent travelers between the ages of 30-45, most of whom have young families. In today's competitive parental environment, "Keeping up with the Joneses" is a big deal. They want the best schools, best clothes, best tennis instructor, etc. The teenage and college age kids of "Orange County Housewives" drive BMW's, shop for Coach Handbags and designer clothes. And when they travel, they want to be the first to experience what's hot in the newest destinations and cruises.

"The Real Housewives of Orange County" is a reality show that that gives us a glimpse of travelers that want the most luxurious travel experience so that they can come back with the stories to tell of where they have been. This lifestyle may not be mine or yours, but it doesn't mean that you can't be their "travel concierge." Find ways to target your marketing to the 30 million behind those gated communities. Each gated community has a monthly newsletter or magazines that take advertising. They also hold many social events and offer sponsorship opportunities. Find ways to break through those gates and sell them the "Bragging Rights."

Find ways to target your marketing to 30 million behind those gated communities.

Wealthy…BUT NOT STUPID!

I recently spotted a billboard along the freeway that said "Just because I was born rich doesn't mean I'm stupid." statement really struck a chord with me as I thought back to when I made the decision to move across town, which in the past had been an area that was less than desirable.

A smart developer with a vision purchased a large amount of acreage in the hills with the intent to develop a gated community that would surround a new golf course. Back then this section of town was comprised mostly of low income housing that was surrounded by undeveloped rolling hills and rural farm land.

With just one visit to the development and I knew instantly this had much more than anything that I had previously seen or was even looking for…security, beautiful setting on a golf course, a spa, pool, fitness center and other Country Club amenities!

Because this was a new development in a virtually undeveloped area, the pricing was very attractive. I found a comparable condo unit in the middle of town in the same price category, but it did not come close to matching any of the extra amenities the condo in the development would include. I decided to stretch a bit beyond my budget and go for it.

The lessons I learned next were real eye openers. Since it was a brand new unit, there was only dirt in the small patio outside my back door, surrounded by a short fence. I called for several estimates to have a flagstone patio laid down and was shocked at the quotes I was getting for such a small area. I started asking around my neighbors and they were finding the same thing.

We started to call it "Gate Pricing." You would get a rough estimate by phone, and then, as soon as they came through the gates and saw the golf course and country club the price seemed to double or sometimes triple. This started happening every time I called for any type of services. I am certain that if I had bought that the same price basic condo in the middle of town the quotes would have been more in line with what would be reasonable.

Since this was a new community in the hills, there also weren't any grocery stores or shopping centers close by. Of course, it wasn't too long before another "dollar signs-in-the-eyes" developer bought some adjacent property and built a strip mall. He believed he struck gold and didn't want just any stores, he wanted only "high-end" establishments - and charged rent accordingly.

Again, the assumption was that everyone who lived within the community would clamor to spend their money there, if only for the convenience. Well, one by one, the establishments opened and subsequently closed down. The rent the businesses were being charged was so exorbitant that they had no choice but to overcharge for their products. The specialty grocery store had to lay off employees, the boutique toy store went out of business and the chic restaurant had to liquidate everything including the fixtures and the complete inventory of expensive liquor. We were left with real estate companies and mortgage brokers.

Thank goodness they kept the Starbucks! At least the neighbors can still pick up their non-fat, decaf, no-foam lattes for their road trip to the nearest Costco, which happens to be about 15 miles away!

You see, even the wealthy will drive a few extra miles to spend their money at Costco, not because they have to, but because they choose to. With competitive prices on everyday goods, high-quality items and brand-name products, Costco attracts smart, affluent people. And bigger spenders results in bigger revenue for Costco. *Hmmm…* Competitive pricing for high quality products. Add to this formula exceptional personal service and there's the key to selling luxury travel to the wealthy.

Learning from my experiences, I slowly and steadily I penetrated my sales into the community by using various ongoing and consistent communication tactics, such as ads in the community newsletter, listing on the club's website, ads in the member directory and other neighbor's testimonials. And I knew first and foremost that I had to gain their trust by assuring them that I had their best interest in mind – and not what was in their bank accounts.

Many of those "dollar-sign-in-the-eyes" companies that targeted our new community did get our business. However, when they were paid in full most of them were "gone with the wind" leaving us high and dry with no recourse.

With patience, hard work, and determination, eventually my travel business gained recognition, and I have established a comfort level among my high-end customers, who know that I am truly legitimate and not just another "Fly-By-Night-Travel.com."

DIARY OF A LUXURY TRAVEL AGENT

Dear Diary:

8:00AM: It's early Sunday morning and I have an appointment at 5:00PM at my clients' home to go over their upcoming trip to Greece and Turkey. It's a little over a month before they leave on their trip, and this is normally the time when clients start to really think about the vacation that we may have planned months ago.

> *Here's a typical day in the life of a high-end travel planner.*

I have also realized when looking at my calendar that I have a deadline today for an article on selling luxury travel. I decided it would be best to work on my client's presentation before writing the article since I know that it will take me time to create a personalized handbook on their upcoming trip. The article will have to take second priority today.

8:30AM: I scour my files for reference material on Greece and Turkey. I look for my notes on the trip I made to Athens earlier that same year. I search the web for more information and pictures to include in the material. I cut, copy and paste any pertinent data on all of the five-star hotels they will be staying at, as well as on the cruise that they will be taking.

9:30AM: Just finished creating a custom personalized full-color cover insert to slip in the front of the binder. The title says "Prepared especially for Mr. and Mrs. Christensen." Also included in this cover sheet are the names of each island they will visit in vertical bullet points along the side. I incorporated beautiful pictures of Greece and, of course, I included my name, logo and agency information.

10:00AM: Inside the "Greek Blue" colored binder I purchased, I have inserted fold out maps of each cities and islands that they will visit during their stay and four-day cruise. Each destination in the trip has a section and a tab for easy reference. I have also included my personal packing tips, cruise advice, hotel information, transportation guides, tour and restaurant suggestions, emergency contact information, copies of itineraries to leave at home and extra copies of their passports. I will also let them know that I will keep a copy of their passports and they can feel free to call me at any time should they lose them. I have enclosed copies of the letters that I composed to send on their behalf to every hotel manager of each hotel that they will be staying. They will now have the hotel manager's name should any problems arise.

Competitive pricing for high-quality products. Add to this formula exceptional personal service, and that's the key to selling luxury travel to the wealthy

12:00PM: I have finally completed *"The Book."* Putting all of this together has taken me about four hours.

4:00PM: I am now putting together a gift basket that includes a bottle of Greek wine I purchased on my last trip to Athens and a beautiful table top book showing all the gorgeous views to help them get excited about their upcoming trip.

5:00PM: It was a delightful surprise when I arrived at my clients' home to find out that there were other couples there for a pool party and dinner. Everyone wanted to see what I had brought over and they were quite impressed with all of the detail and effort that I had put into their trip. As they all shared a glass of the Greek wine I brought, everyone was intrigued to hear all about the trip. They also expressed amazement that I would come out and make this type of presentation on a Sunday!!!

As it turned out, I came home with the names and phones numbers of several prospective clients. As a matter of fact, I was asked by a couple of the dinner guests to call them next week to help them plan some upcoming trips. What I have learned is that if you treat your clients with special care and extra attention, they will repay you with a wealth of referrals.

7:00PM – Finally back home! Not bad for a day's work…even if it was Sunday.

7:15PM - Dear Diary, What about my article on selling luxury travel?…Done! I realized that this day says it all. I think I'll sleep in tomorrow.

I have also provided all of the travel services for several group golf trips for this same client. He mentioned on this particular day that he wanted me to start planning the next trip to Puerto Vallarta. The first golf trip I put together for him earned me nearly $10,000.00 in commissions. In addition, his wife is the local Rotary Club President, which gave me the opportunity to send a contingency of members to the annual convention in Copenhagen.

"If you are serious about dealing with affluent travelers, you must first understand that time is what they lack the most".

But give up a Sunday, you say? You bet I will!!! If you are serious about dealing with affluent travelers you must first understand that time is what they lack the most. Making the travel planning process as carefree and effortless as possible will cement your relationship and value to them. By meeting the clients on their schedule and convenience, will give you an opportunity to sit down with them to make sure you have met their expectations and provide any additional guidance or services that they may require.

Chapter 23 | POWER AFTER THOUGHTS

TAKE YOUR PASSION TO PROFIT

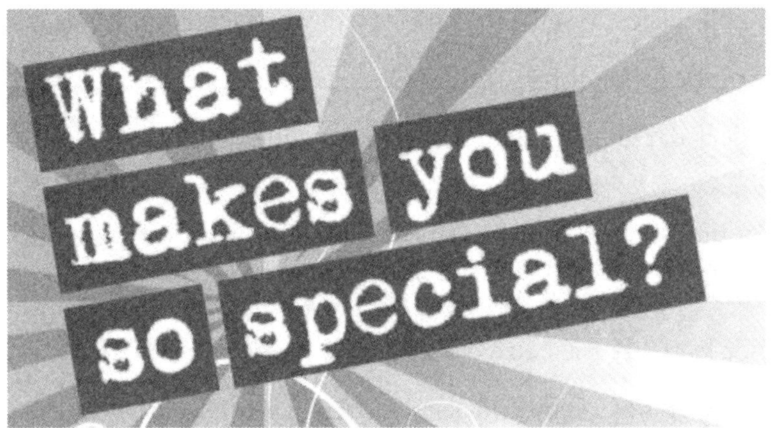

Understanding what makes you special and knowing how to promote yourself and develop great relationships with clients will help you become your own home-based powerhouse.

At a business networking group meeting I attended recently, the group's president offered an "icebreaker" question: "What would each of you do if you had just won the lottery?" One by one, everyone else said without hesitation that they would travel. There was one exception: a person who said she would buy a ranch, raise cattle and crops…and then she would travel!

I grinned from ear to ear and thought, "I'm the one who just won the lottery!" And my luck continued as I was last to get up and introduce myself. I knew that this icebreaker question had opened up a huge marketing opportunity for me. I also knew I needed to be warm, engaging and genuine.

I started out by saying, "Wow! I just realized how much I truly love my job. I'm so happy that I'm here today so that I can let everyone know that I'm the one person who can make all of your travel dreams come true. I would be thrilled to be your travel concierge and take care of all of the planning and preparation for your trip of a lifetime. I work with every budget, and with my special services and expert guidance you won't have to win the lottery to be treated like a millionaire." I went on to explain specifically why it would benefit them to use my services.

So how can you build relationships with a room full of complete strangers like that? Here are a few tips:

Build your confidence – I've had travel agents tell me that they can provide every fact about a cruise line or destination, but crumble at the idea of getting up to talk about what they're good at. The fact is that we all basically sell the same travel products at comparable prices. So it becomes crucial that you become comfortable when explaining what will make booking travel with you a special experience in contrast to booking online or booking direct.

Create a script – If you have trouble talking about yourself or stumble on your words, create a script or bullet points that you can keep with you or by the phone at all times. This script can be used with any customer lead. If I asked you right now why I should book my travel with you, what would your answer be? Can you list five top reasons why you're so special?

Promote your experience – How many cruises have you been on? How many countries have you visited? How many FAM trips have you been on? By relating your experiences, you create trust with your clients that you're capable of handling their trip based on your personal knowledge.

Communicate with clients – As the travel planning process develops, assure your clients that you will keep in touch, even if it's just to let them know that you're still working on their trip.

Be an advocate – Talk about what you've done for other customers to avert or solve any travel mishaps. Let your clients know up front that you will always be available for them and will fight like heck to be their advocate should something go wrong. Remind them that when they book online that they won't have such support.

> *Building relationships with customers should be the most important way for you to build business.*

Show your passion – Express your excitement about working with your clients and let your passion shine through. Bring your sense of humor into your conversation. Clients like dealing with someone who's happy and upbeat.

Provide a sense of security – Encourage your clients to always carry your business card with them wherever they travel and remind them that they're free to call you at any time. This gives them an assurance that you will be there for them and provides an extra feeling of security.

Go the extra mile – Do you send a VIP letter introducing your clients to hotel managers? Do you offer gift baskets? When you send them their documents, make sure that you let your clients know they will be receiving something special on their trip.

Develop customer relationships – Think about the last best customer service experience you received. Figure out what made it so special and then try to replicate it in your business model. Building relationships with customers should be the most important way for you to build your business. How customers feel about their anticipated travel experience when booking with a travel agent affects what they tell others about us. It has a significant impact not just on our reputation, but ultimately on the growth of our business. Indeed, word of mouth is how I built my business… one customer relationship at a time.

References | RESOURCES

For Anita Pagliasso's other books and products:

WWW.TRAVELAGENTATHOME.COM

WWW.REDTICKETPRODUCTIONS.COM

WWW.ATICKET2TRAVEL.COM

Agent@Home Magazine – www.agentathome.com

Anita Pagliasso writes the monthly "Working At Home" column for this magazine. Agent@Home is the only publication devoted exclusively to helping home-based agents successfully manage their at-home business. Sign up for a Free Subscription by going to www.agentathome.com

Career Quest - http://www.careerquesttraining.com/

Career Quest, unlike many other online schools, specializes in training for travel careers. They provide the technical training and skills you need to work as a home based agent or a retail travel agent.

Career Quest Online Programs:

New Enhanced Online Curriculum!

- Home-based Travel Agent
- Independent Contractor Travel Agent
- Cruise Consultant
- Retail Travel Agent
- Travel Associate

Kelly Monaghan, CTC - www. HomeTravelAgency.com

Becoming A Travel Agent – The Home-Based Travel Agent Resource Center

Working at home in your own home-based travel agency is one of the most exciting business opportunities available to the home-based entrepreneur. It can be done full-**time, part-time,** on a regular basis or just occasionally. It's really up to you how you choose to define your home-based business.

Becoming a travel agent is actually very easy. Yet it is difficult to get reliable, unbiased information about how to start, operate, and succeed in your home-based travel agency. There are competing points of view, differences of opinion, and clashing agendas at work. There has also been a great deal of misinformation passed around, in the press and on the Internet, about what a home-based travel agent is and is not.

That's why Kelly set up this site and created a Home Study Course, providing you with factual and unbiased information.

Keith Powell – The Business Revivalist

Reviving business will require tossing out the stagnant, giving something new a try and learning in the process. Keith will help you transform your business with renewed creativity, purpose and focus.

Powell is known as the Business Revivalist, specializing in the travel industry. He provides assistance in developing business plans, marketing plans and can guide you with new creative ideas to grow your travel business. Helping entrepreneurs has been Keith's passion for over 30 years. Contact Keith at powellspeaks@gmail.com or visit www.keithpowellspeaker.com

PATH – www.PATH4hosts.com

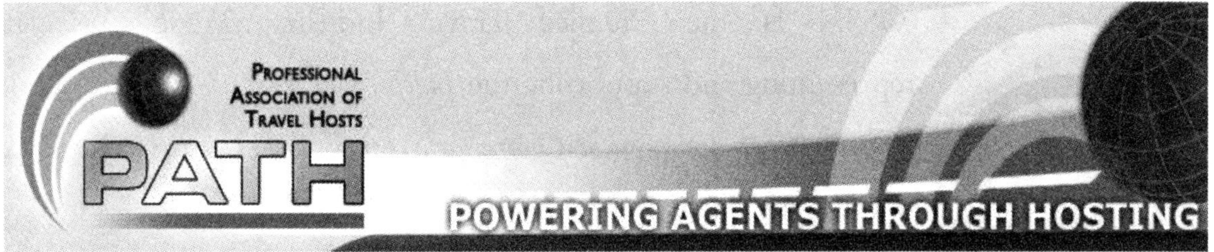

The Professional Association of Travel Hosts, Inc. (PATH) is a non-partisan corporation, with a membership comprised of credible U.S. Host Agencies.

The concept of the Host Agency has blossomed significantly in the past years flourishing into an array of business models that have confused what a Host Agency truly is. This has resulted in the need for a professional society of Host Agencies that want to establish operating standards with strict enforcement among its members.

The purpose of PATH is:

- To establish a Code of Ethics and Performance Standards for Host Agencies
- To bring educational and training opportunities to its members and their Affiliated Travel Agents
- To further communications between the Host Agency members, its Affiliates and Travel Suppliers

For more information on host agencies, go to www.PATH4Hosts.com

SATH – www.sath.org

The Society for Accessible Travel & Hospitality (SATH), founded in 1976, is an educational nonprofit membership organization whose mission is to raise awareness of the needs of all travelers with disabilities, remove physical and attitudinal barriers to free access and expand travel opportunities in the United States and abroad. Members include travel professionals, consumers with disabilities and other individuals and corporations who support our mission.

OSSN – www.ossn.com

OSSN is the Premier Travel Industry Trade Association representing and supporting the *Independent Travel Agents, Home Based Travel Agency, Independent Contractor Seller of Travel and the Outside Sales Travel Agent.*

OSSN's mission is to provide our members with every possible tool and unlimited travel agent training to help their business succeed in today's new travel environment. OSSN provides members with a variety of educational programs and networking communication platforms that allow members a professional forum to help ENSURE the success of your travel agent business.

The Outside Sales Support Network was founded in 1990. Today our travel Association is has over 80 Chapters with over 8000 members and more than 200 Allied Supplier Members.

The "Members Only" section of this site is designed to help your home-based travel agency with over 6500 pages with in depth information that is guaranteed to help your travel agency prosper.

Look for the special discount for readers of From Home-Based to Powerhouse on the next page.

Special OSSN Membership offer for the readers of

<u>From Home-Based to POWERHOUSE</u>

$25.00 Discount for a one-year OSSN Membership.

The total price is only $130.00 (Priced normally at $155)

Please copy, complete and fax this application to 1-408-532-0872

Name of Applicant____

Home Address____

City________________________________ State______ Zip________________

Phone (   )____________________________ Fax (   )____________________

E-mail Address ____

If Applicable

IATAN #_________________________CLIA #___________________________

Credit Card_______________________Exp.___________Total$_____________

Signature___________________________________Date:________________

Membership agreement and statement of liability. Membership is valid from one year from the date of application. Renewal fees are $105.00 and are subject to change without notice. Member fees are non-refundable. Travel Support Systems, Inc. DBA Outside Sales Support Network neither guarantees nor insures the services provided by any officer, employee or member and shall assume no responsibility to liability for actions beyond its own control in connection with services provided. OSSN is not responsible for any act, error, omission, injury, loss, accident, nonperformance or any other irregularity, or any consequences resulting there from, which may be occasional through neglect, default or any other action of association/company, carrier or person engages in the service of OSSN.

Please submit questions and application to:

Outside Sales Support Network
Western Regional Office
5453 Silver Vista Way, San Jose, Ca., 95138
Phone 408-531-9228 Fax 408-532-0872
westernregion@ossn.com

Bonus | SAMPLE LETTERS AND NOTES

"I'm in the Travel Business" Letter

It is with a great deal of pleasure that I am announcing that I am now in the travel business. I am extremely fortunate to be working with an agency that has twelve years experience in the travel industry. (List any other credentials of the agency here.)

I hope to be of help to you with any of your travel needs, whether it be an ocean cruise, a romantic honeymoon, a business trip, a much deserved vacation or a trip to Europe. I will take care of every detail for you, including car rentals and hotel reservations. I will be more than happy to deliver all of your travel documents to your home or office.

If you are thinking of a trip anywhere, give me a call. I will get you brochures and literature for the destination you have in mind. I have access to all the most current travel bargains available so you can get the most for your hard earned money.

I can't tell you how excited I am about my new adventure. My passion for travel and my experience at event planning make this new career a perfect fit. I look forward to making your travel dreams a reality and creating many wonderful memories for you.

Sincerely,

"Thank you for your Business" Note

Thank you for your business and your "Vote of Confidence"

I recognize you have many choices when it comes to travel service providers, therefore, I'm honored that you have given me the opportunity to serve you and fulfill your travel dreams.

I look forward to helping you plan your travel for many more years to come.

Please accept my sincere appreciation.

Follow Up Letter

Dear

Thank you for giving (name of agency) the opportunity to make your travel arrangements for your recent trip to (destination)

We hope that you were pleased with the (example: air travel and the hotel accommodations) that we arranged for you. We encourage your comments, insofar as that is the best means that we have for learning first hand if the representations of quality that are made to us are accurate.

We will look forward to hearing from you and hope that you will afford us the opportunity to help you plan your next vacation or business trip.

Thank you,

Sample VIP Client Letter

Hotel
Address
Attention: Hotel or General Manager
Phone:
Fax:

Regarding: (Supplier) reservation number _________ for (Client's name)
Arrival: Month/day/year
Departure: Month/day/year

Dear

The above reservations are for VIP clients of my agency. I recommended your property to them based on my confidence that you will make sure their visit to (LOCATION) will be a most elegant and enjoyable experience for them.

My clients, Mr. and Mrs. Traveler, will be celebrating their (anniversary, birthday, reunion, etc.) during their stay with you.

I have requested for them an (ocean view, non-smoking room with a king-size bed). Their flight arrives in (LOCATION) at (TIME) so they may require an early check in. It is also my understanding that included with their stay will be (EXAMPLE: Daily full American breakfast for 2 and unlimited domestic beverages.)

I would appreciate your personal attention to this reservation. Please confirm that the hotel has the booking information correct and, if at all possible, provide them with any additional complimentary upgrades available.

I would like to thank you in advance for making my clients feel very special and welcome. You can be assured that I will continue to recommend your beautiful hotel to all of my clients and groups.

An early reply to this fax would be greatly appreciated.

Thank you for personally taking care of my important clients.

Regards,

cc: file, clients

Letter to Pied Piper or Group Travel Leader

LEARN HOW TO TRAVEL FOR FREE

Experience the world of free travel. Our "**Pied Piper Program**" was developed for those of you who work, play and associate with others who love to travel.

Have you ever thought of escorting a tour or going on a cruise with a group of friends and family? It's simple...just determine where YOU would like to go and start recruiting. Before you know it you have a **FREE** trip!

Here is how the Pied Piper Program works for a free cruise:

- With the help of one of our travel specialists, you will select a cruise, along with a date for travel.
- Ticket To Travel then obtains the best possible group rate from the cruise line.
- You recruit 15 people to go on the same cruise and you will get a FREE BERTH.
- If you get 16 couples in a group you will get a FREE CABIN.

Here's how Ticket To Travel will assist you:

- We handle all the bookings with the cruise line.
- We provide flyers and brochures for you to give potential group members.
- We provide step-by-step helps as you work with your group.
- We handle all of the paper work and collection of payments.
- We will inform the group of the travel schedule and final details.

Note: The program will be similar for any other type of group travel packages.

Index |INDEX

Notes |NOTES

Notes | NOTES